THE
OPERA NEWS
BOOK OF
FIGARO

THE
OPERA NEWS
BOOK
OF *Figaro*

Edited by Frank Merkling

ILLUSTRATED

DODD, MEAD & COMPANY · NEW YORK

Library of Congress Catalog Card Number: 67-21213
Printed in the United States of America
by The Cornwall Press, Inc., Cornwall, N. Y.

Musical examples courtesy of G. Schirmer, Inc., New York

Contents

Le Nozze di Figaro   1

   The Background
   What to Say
   The Music
   The Story

A Tender Irony by Edward Downes   8
Figaro's Perpetual Motion by Katherine Griffith   16
Mozart's Wedding Symphony
   by Frederick W. Sternfeld   31
Marriages in *Figaro* by Joseph Kerman   38
Master of Human Insight by Tibor Kozma   45
Meet Marcellina by Ann M. Lingg   50
Mooncalves by Mary Watkins Cushing   54
The Clarinet in *Figaro* by Tibor Kozma   58
The Court Jester by Robert Breuer   65
Revolutionary Figaro by Jane W. Stedman   69
The Battle of *Figaro* by Ann M. Lingg   75

Da Ponte and the Bussanis by Lloyd Harris   81

Michael Kelly by Paul Nettl   86

Figaro Dressed for Paris by Christopher Raeburn   97

The Road to *Figaro* by Baird Hastings   104

Mozart after Mardi Gras by Frederick W. Sternfeld   113

The Happy Ending by Frank J. Warnke   124

The Twilight of the Almavivas by William Weaver   129

From Revolution to Romance
   by Alfred Frankenstein   134

Mozart among Us by Max Rudolf   137

Index   141

Illustrations

Following page 22

Mozart, 1789
Beaumarchais
Da Ponte
Joseph II
Antonio Salieri
Beaumarchais's *Le Mariage de Figaro*
Mozart with Maria Theresa and Joseph II
Francesco Benucci
Anna Salina Storace
Dorotea Bussani
Michael Kelly
Mozart, 1782-83
Mozart Monument

Following page 118

Playbill for première of *Le Nozze di Figaro*
The Burgtheater in Vienna
Scene from Act I
Set for Act I

vii

Sketch of Susanna's costume
Scene from Act II
Set for Act II
Finale of Act II
Sketch of Countess's costume
Letter Duet from Act III
The Marriage Ceremony
Set for Act III
Sketch of Figaro's costume
Scene from Act IV
Set for Act IV
Finale of Act IV

THE
OPERA NEWS
BOOK OF
FIGARO

Le Nozze di Figaro

The Background

Wolfgang Amadeus Mozart (Salzburg 1756–Vienna 1791) showed himself a prodigy as early as age four. His father, a composer and well-known violinist, trained and enthusiastically promoted the boy's talent, taking him at six to Vienna, where he and his sister played keyboard concerts and were invited to court by Empress Maria Theresa. Trips to Paris (at seven), England (at eight), and Italy (at fourteen) followed. In Milan the young man conducted twenty consecutive performances of *Mitridate,* his first opera in serious classical style.

As a name in the music world, he had to contend with an all-powerful clique of fashionable Italian opera composers and performers. Uneven fortunes, meeting with his rather gentle nature and his wife's haphazard domestic management, did much to contribute to the composer's overwork and death at thirty-five. Nevertheless, he wrote twenty-five works for the stage.

Like his instrumental music, his operas combine dramatic flair with extreme versatility of form and style. *The Abduction from the Seraglio* and *The Magic Flute*, for example, were the first major operas written in German, and they had spoken dialogue. *Le Nozze di Figaro*, however, features the keyboard-accompanied recitative and vocal dash of Italian opera. While not neglecting the gay ensembles and devices of *opera buffa*, Mozart gave his stock figures music that characterizes them with singular depth and poignancy.

The personage of Figaro had been introduced by French playwright Pierre Augustin Caron, known as Beaumarchais, in his comedy *The Barber of Seville* (1775) and its sequel, *The Marriage of Figaro* (1784). Both plays so satirized the pre-Revolutionary social order that only with difficulty was librettist Lorenzo Da Ponte able to secure Emperor Joseph's clearance for Mozart's version.

First heard at the Vienna Burgtheater on May 1, 1786, the new opera aroused cheers and many calls for encores. But Italians in the cast, led on by an anti-Mozart faction, tried to sabotage the production, bringing *Figaro* to a close after nine performances. Its real success was at Prague, after which Mozart supplied additional arias for the Vienna revival in 1789.

The first known performance in America took place at the Park Theater, New York, on May 10, 1824, in English. The Metropolitan Opera House had been open ten seasons before *Figaro* was first given there—on January 31,

1894, with Emma Eames as the Countess, Lillian Nordica as Susanna, Edouard de Reszke as Almaviva, and Mario Ancona in the title role. Notable productions in our century include those at England's Glyndebourne Festival in 1934 and at the Metropolitan during the 1939–40 season, when Ettore Panizza conducted a cast that included Elisabeth Rethberg, Bidù Sayão, Risë Stevens (Cherubino), John Brownlee, and Ezio Pinza. This became, on December 7, 1940, the first opera broadcast under Texaco sponsorship.

What to Say

Le Nozze di Figaro: Leh *Nought*-seh dee *Fee*-gah-ro
Basilio: Bah-*zeel*-yo
Cherubino: Keh-rue-*bee*-no
Curzio: *Coort*-syo (a lawyer)
Marcellina: Mahr-cheh-*lee*-na

THE MUSIC

FIGARO, SUSANNA: *Cinque, dieci, venti*

FIGARO: *Se vuol ballare*

BARTOLO: *La vendetta*

MARCELLINA, SUSANNA: *Via resti servita*

CHERUBINO: *Non so più cosa son*

COUNT, BASILIO, SUSANNA: *Cosa sento?*

PEASANTS: *Giovani liete*

THE STORY

ACT I. As Figaro, former barber of Seville now in the service of Count Almaviva, and the Countess' pretty maid Susanna prepare the room they will occupy after their impending marriage, Susanna warns Figaro that the Count has amorous designs on her. Figaro angrily vows to outwit Almaviva. When the room is empty, Dr. Bartolo, the Countess' former guardian, enters with his aging housekeeper, Marcellina; still seeking revenge on the man who made him lose his ward to Almaviva, he persuades Marcellina to sue Figaro for breach of promise. Susanna returns and spars with Marcellina, who leaves in a huff. Soon the young page Cherubino comes to ask Susanna's protection from the Count, who found him courting Barbarina, the gardener's daughter. After confessing that he is "in love with love," the boy hides as Almaviva arrives. The approach of the music master Don Basilio, however, causes the Count, too, to hide. At Basilio's insinuations that Cherubino loves the Countess, the Count steps forth; reenacting how he found the page with Barbarina, he again discovers Cherubino. Amid the ensuing confusion Figaro leads in a group of peasants. They extol the benevolence of Almaviva, who drafts Cherubino into his regiment and departs with the others. Figaro teases Cherubino about army life.

ACT II. In her boudoir the Countess laments her husband's fading love. With Susanna and Figaro she plots to chasten him: Cherubino, disguised as Susanna, will meet with the Count, who will then be caught red-handed. Cherubino, who comes to bid the Countess farewell with a song in praise of love, is disguised by Susanna in girl's clothes. Hearing her husband approach while the maid is out of the room, the Countess locks Cherubino in a closet; when the jealous Almaviva hears a noise inside, he leaves (with his wife) to secure tools to break the lock. Susanna, who has overheard, helps Cherubino escape through the window and takes his place, completely baffling the Count on his return. All seem relieved until the gardener Antonio enters to complain that someone has jumped into his flower bed. Unaware of what has happened, Figaro takes the blame, but the Count proves hard to convince. Marcellina, Bartolo, and Basilio burst in with a court summons for Figaro, to the delight of Almaviva.

ACT III. In the palace audience room, Susanna promises the Count a rendezvous, but he suspects a ruse when he overhears

FIGARO: *Non più andrai*

COUNTESS: *Porgi, amor*

CHERUBINO: *Voi che sapete*

SUSANNA: *Venite, inginocchiatevi*

SUSANNA, CHERUBINO: *Aprite, presto aprite*
ANTONIO: *Ah! signor!*

FIGARO: *Sono io stesso saltato di li*

COUNT, SUSANNA: *Crudel! perchè finora*

THE MUSIC

COUNT: *Vedrò mentr'io sospiro*

COUNTESS: *Dove sono*
COUNTESS, SUSANNA: *Che soave zefiretto*

PEASANTS: *Ricevete, o padroncina*

WEDDING MARCH

BARBARINA: *L'ho perduta*

FIGARO: *Aprite un po' quegli occhi*

SUSANNA: *Deh! vieni, non tardar*

CHERUBINO: *Pian pianin le andrò più presso*

THE STORY

her laughing with Figaro, he vows revenge. Marcellina arrives to demand that Figaro pay his debts or marry her at once but soon discovers he is her long-lost natural son, fathered by Bartolo. The Countess enters; alone onstage, she mourns her lost love. To further the conspiracy she dictates a note for Susanna to sign, inviting the Count to the garden. Peasant girls, among them the disguised Cherubino, now bring flowers to their lady. Just as the page is discovered by Almaviva, the wedding processions of Figaro and Susanna and of Bartolo and Marcellina advance. During the festivities, Susanna slips the note to the Count.

ACT IV. In the moonlit garden Barbarina has lost the pin the Count has given her in reply to Susanna's note. After she tells Figaro and Marcellina of the secret assignation, Figaro delivers a tirade against womankind and leaves. Susanna and the Countess appear, dressed in each other's gowns; dropping her disguise for a moment, Susanna rhapsodizes on her love for Figaro, who, overhearing her, thinks she refers to the Count. Susanna hides. Next the Countess, protesting, is wooed by Cherubino, who mistakes her for Susanna. This angers the

Count, who chases the page away and sends the disguised Countess ahead to an arbor. He then disappears. By now Figaro has caught on and makes exaggerated love to Susanna, who, believing he loves the Countess, boxes his ears. But the couple is quickly reconciled, pretending when the Count returns that Figaro has won the Countess. Just as the outraged husband calls everyone to bear witness, the Countess reveals herself. Grasping the truth at last, Almaviva begs his wife's pardon; all are happily united.

FIGARO, SUSANNA: *Eccomi a' vostri piedi*

COUNT: *Gente, gente! all'armi!*

COUNT: *Contessa, perdono!*

A Tender Irony

BY EDWARD DOWNES

What is the magic that makes Mozart's *Marriage of Figaro* bewitchingly youthful? It is so fresh that no one ever thinks of calling it "young for its age," though *Figaro* is nearly two centuries old—the oldest opera in the standard repertory. The answer is Mozart's genius for characterization. Goethe once said that there is no deep understanding without love. The deeper answer to our question lies in Mozart's love of human nature.

When we see spoken dramas of Mozart's epoch—Schiller's tremendous *Don Carlos,* say, or a comedy, Sheridan's *School for Scandal,* even Beaumarchais's *Mariage de Figaro,* on which Mozart's opera is based—we are apt to call them "amazingly modern," by which we mean that their joints don't creak as much as we expected. But *Figaro* always seems as light-footed as the rapscallion Cherubino, jumping out the window of the Countess' boudoir, bouncing off the ground below and away so fast that the gardener never sees his face.

What is this beguiling resilience of spirit and feeling, as well as action and interaction of characters? Is it in the play? No; Beaumarchais's characters lack both the depth and the subtlety of Mozart's. Beaumarchais's play is satirical and revolutionary in intent. Napoleon once said that in it one could already hear the cannon of the French Revolution. But Beaumarchais's boom is dated; the battle is won; and the play, with all its brilliance, is a period piece.

Mozart's revolution was a very different one. His *Nozze di Figaro* was the first opera to present a group of "real" characters, characters portrayed in the round and psychologically in depth. And he was the first composer to make his drama develop out of the clash of these personalities. If their strength did not come from the play, was it perhaps the poetry of Mozart's librettist? Again the answer is no; Da Ponte was much more than the average librettist, but he was not a distinguished poet. The sharpness and depth of Mozart's characters come from the music. Whether we take a secondary character, like the page Cherubino, or a dominating one, like Count Almaviva, we find his profile firmly etched in Mozart's melodic line.

There are opera-lovers who are disturbed at the idea of having the part of a young page sung by a woman. But this is no mere operatic convention. It was Beaumarchais himself who specified that the role of Chérubin "can only be acted, as it was acted [at the premiere], by a young and very pretty woman; we have no young men in our theaters sufficiently trained to catch the finesse of this role." It

was the Danish philosopher Kierkegaard who remarked
that Cherubino is Don Giovanni as a boy. Young enough
to have a soprano voice, old enough to be thrown into the
most delicious confusion by each pretty feminine face,
Cherubino describes his state in his first little aria, "Non
so più," which he sings to Susanna. Every woman, he says,
makes his heart flutter, and the flutter is there in the
breathless little repetitive rhythms of his opening phrase,
"I hardly know who I am or what I am doing":

Non so   più   co - sa   son,   co - sa   fac - cio,

By the subtle device of introducing the sensuous tone of
the clarinet for the first time in Cherubino's aria, Mozart
adds a telling touch to this portrait. The clarinet also returns in Cherubino's second aria, "Voi che sapete," an
equally sensuous though more courtly love lyric, which
he performs for both the Countess and Susannna.

Cherubino's opposite pole is Count Almaviva, a man of
powerful passions who is determined to possess his wife's
pretty maid. His rage when he discovers Cherubino hiding in Susanna's room under seemingly compromising
circumstances is exceeded only by his jealous fury when
he believes he has trapped the page in the Countess's room.
She protests the boy's innocence in agitated, pleading
phrases. The Count's only reply is to demand the key to
her room with an arrogance and passion bordering on
brutality:

Quà   la   chia-ve!

There is an almost savage quality to the Count's exclamation "Mora, mora!" (He shall die, he shall die!).

In Act III the Count feels himself painfully wounded when he discovers that Susanna has not only pretended to make a rendezvous with him but is actually plotting against him with her fiancé Figaro. Though enraged at the discovery that Susanna does not intend to give herself to him, Almaviva finds even more painful the thought that a mere servant of his, Figaro, should be happy with her (as her husband) while he, the great Count, must sigh in vain. His aria, "Vedrò mentre io sospiro" (Shall I see, while I sigh in vain), expresses not only his rage, in the many emphatic leaps culminating in the upward jump of a tenth on the word *audace,* but the torment of wounded pride in the

tu   non   na-sce-sti,au - da - ce,

chromatic climb of the subsequent phrase.

Figaro, alerted to the Count's designs on Susanna in the first scene of the opera, can allow himself no such outbursts of temper, but he is confident that in the approaching battle of wits he will worst his master. His feelings of ironical superiority and bitter resentment are fused through Mozart's incredible virtuosity into a seemingly simple tune. Only the persistently repeated notes, which return again and again throughout the aria, suggest the ominous threat behind Figaro's words:

Se vuol bal - la - re,   si - gnor Con - ti - no,

There is similar irony in his "Non più andrai," which he sings to Cherubino after the page has been ordered away to join the army. Figaro is delighted that Cherubino will no longer be around to pay unwelcome attentions to Susanna, and he bids him a mocking farewell, describing the military glories that await him.

Only in Act IV does Figaro momentarily lose his self-possession—when he believes that Susanna actually *is* betraying him with the Count. Figaro's "Aprite un po' quegli occhi," denouncing all womankind for their perfidy and cruelty to men, is often dismissed as a brilliant but conventional *opera buffa* aria on a conventional topic, addressed to the audience in conventional comic style. But it would be most unlike Mozart, at this crucial point in a work on which he had lavished such loving skill, to fall back on mere formulas, no matter how skillfully he could manipulate them. Actually, this aria—with its stabbing accents, drastic repeated phrases and rhythms, whirling triplets and climbing pitch—can sound like the panic outburst of a man who has almost lost control of himself.

Susanna, who is wooed throughout the opera by three men—the Count, Cherubino, and Figaro—is more quick-witted than any of them. Her love and unswerving loyalty

go to Figaro, of course, but she is piqued by his jealousy
and resolves to teach him a lesson. After Figaro's aria she
comes to the garden and pretends to be waiting for the
Count. There she sings "Deh! vieni, non tardar," an out-
wardly simple serenade sung to the joy of her heart. The
ambiguity of the situation is that Figaro imagines the
momentary joy of her heart to be the Count; we know,
however, that she has no use for the Count and that the
delicate ardor of this aria could only be directed toward
her true beloved. It is Figaro, not the audience, who mis-
understands the tender invitation of a phrase like the following:

Vie - ni, ben mi - o, tra que - ste pian-te a - sco - se,

There are many other sides to Susanna's character, which
show in her duets with Figaro and the Countess. In some
of the ensemble scenes where the Countess and Susanna
are allied against the Count, the two women's parts run
together sometimes in parallel thirds, sometimes in parallel
sixths—in anxiety when the plot takes an unfavorable turn,
or in happy teasing of the Count when they are triumphant.

Though the Countess shares many characteristics with
Susanna as long as they are two faithful women allied
against a philandering Count, the Countess's dominating
trait is an affectionate melancholy. This she shares with no
one else in the cast, and this is what brings her near to our

heart. Her two arias, "Porgi, amor" and "Dove sono," express unwavering love and tenderness for her husband and sadness at the loss of his affection:

One feels here the warmth of Mozart's own love for his Countess. But Mozart's affections were wide. His attitude toward all his characters was one of understanding, but he could see them enough from the outside to feel a tender irony. He could even feel tenderness for the ignoble Count. At the end of the opera, when the Count's philandering has been exposed and he has been thoroughly humiliated, he experiences a change of heart. He, who refused forgiveness to the Countess when he believed her guilty, now falls to his knees before his wife and asks her pardon in such moving tones that we are convinced he has some nobility of soul after all. It is as if he had taken on something of the warmth and humanity of his wife:

This moment is a comparatively unimportant one in Beaumarchais's original play, and there is nothing even in the libretto to indicate that Da Ponte thought it important. But Mozart makes of it an unforgettable high point of the opera.

In the end it is Mozart's affection for all his characters,

the sinners as well as the saints, which moves us so deeply
and makes the characters so deeply "real." When the curtain falls on the last act, as Alfred Einstein says, we are
"by no means satisfied in regard to the future marital happiness of the poor Countess, but we know in this work
Mozart has added to the world's understanding of people
and its lightness of spirit."

Figaro's Perpetual Motion

BY KATHERINE GRIFFITH

If *The Marriage of Figaro* can be said to have one pre-dominant quality, a trait characteristic of both the play and the operatic setting, it is perpetual motion. Nothing stands still; the moments of poise are rare, and come as an unexpected relief in a plot of constant and highly concentrated action. An entire evening's entertainment could be made of the events of the finale of the second act alone! Confusion piles upon confusion; half a dozen miniature plots arise, come to a climax, are resolved or left at a moment of crisis.

Yet in all the confusion and mercurial speed of dramatic complications, there is order. Music is, inevitably, highly organized; order in sound is its essence. Mozart's own comment was that although in certain dramatic situations the music might appear to forget itself and overstep formal bounds, it must never cease to be music. Form and text work hand in hand. So, in *Figaro*, even while sustaining the perpetual motion, adding to the excitement of the countless crises, portraying mood and character, and covering a great deal of action, the music remains music, clear and satisfying from the formal point of view.

Everything is functional in *Figaro*. Pity the poor director who finds it necessary to shorten the show! The omission of any ensemble is dramatically impossible, for each one is necessary to the continuity of the story. The arias, so often points of rest and commentary in the eighteenth century, are vital to our knowledge of the characters. We would never completely know Figaro without the dancing satire of "Se vuol ballare," the buoyant horseplay of "Non più andrai," and the bitterness of "Aprite un po' quegl' occhi." Each shows a different vein in his personality, and without any one he would be far less human. The Countess, far too well-bred to open her heart in company, shows us its full tenderness and complexity in her two soliloquies, musical portraits of a mature and infinitely interesting personality. Cherubino's youthful effusions are musically youthful, too; comparison of his rhythmically naïve melodies with the more varied ones of the Countess will give the clue to character immediately. Susanna, after three acts of musical bouncing—the patter-like staccato line which is her favorite form of speech—reveals an entirely different side of her nature in "Deh! vieni, non tardar."

At one point in the opera, an aria performs the function of an ensemble. This is Susanna's song in Act II which calls for a great deal of action and is dramatically a duet with Cherubino. Performing this aria in a solo concert would make no more sense than performing the violin part of a trio alone! The point of the piece is its action, the working out of Cherubino's disguise, and Cherubino must do the greater share of the acting. Experienced in stage timing, Mozart allowed just enough time for Susanna to complete the disguise easily before directing Cherubino to walk around the room. Less repetition of text or shorter orchestral interludes would have rushed the actors; more would have created static moments. The importance of this sense of timing is obvious to anyone who has tried to stage *The Old Maid and the Thief,* where the same problem appears in reverse: the thief must be undressed. Unfortunately Menotti, writing especially for radio, allowed so little time to do the things specified by the text that the poor thief usually emerges bruised and breathless in stage performance.

For the most part, the pace and continuity of *Figaro* depend on the ensembles. Of the action-filled finales, much has been said; certainly they are unique in their time as examples of continuous musical and dramatic texture. It is in the shorter ensembles, however—the duets and trios, and the remarkable sextet—that Mozart gives some of his surest strokes of characterization and musical humor.

What does the music do, in an ensemble, besides simply being music? It may tell us that two or more people are present, giving us an idea of their characters or their various states of mind; it may indicate the relationship of these people to one another; it may—and in the skilled

composer, certainly will—reflect the progress of the drama
and suggest any important stage action. The importance
of these duties will vary with the situation, but some of
each element will be present in any well-written ensemble.
By repetition of text—a phenomenon taken for granted in
music, though not in spoken drama—the composer may
emphasize certain ideas above others or may give several
meanings to one sentence. He is in much stronger control
of the inflection of the actors (and, thus, the significance of
the text) than the playwright, even the one who fills his
works with colorful stage directions. The stage direction
of the music itself is the actor's most valuable aid.

The opening duet between Figaro and Susanna tells us
musically something about Figaro (that once he has an
idea, it is hard to change his mind), something about Susanna (that her nature is cheerful, playful but persuasive),
and something about the action onstage (that it involves
starting from a fixed point and reaching farther and farther—in this case, measuring the room):

Another revelation, and the most important here, is the
relationship between Figaro and Susanna. We find them
in disagreement, melodically as well as dramatically, over
which is the more important, the arrangement of the furni-
ture or Susanna's new hat. These two ideas will never mix,
throughout their married life; if Mozart had believed so,

he would have designed the two melodies as counterpoints to each other.

The disagreement is only a minor one, however. Both themes are in the same key, and there is no violent clash of character. It takes a little persistence, but Susanna eventually wins Figaro over to her idea and her melody:

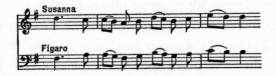

All is well. The bridal couple is singing in parallel thirds and sixths; they love each other and their agreement is perfect—and it is important to the story that we know this. It is the sureness and naturalness of their love which makes the rift between the Count and Countess all the more poignant, assures the success of the plots against the Count, and gives credibility and humor to the fury of each of the lovers when the other is supposedly unfaithful.

In contrast, the second duet shows Figaro and Susanna in a disagreement more serious. "Doubts and suspicions chill me," he says, while she protests, "Your suspicions wrong me." The musical lines disagree as well, first in rhythm:

and then by moving in opposite directions:

The portrayal of character is the main concern of the trio in Act I. The ensemble is set off by a moment of crisis: Basilio, hinting to Susanna that Cherubino's infatuation for the Countess is becoming obvious, is suddenly confronted by the Count, while Cherubino himself listens, concealed in the armchair. This is the Count's first musical appearance, and we are aware of his personality immediately—commanding, accustomed to being obeyed without question, forceful to the point of abruptness, as his accompaniment tells us:

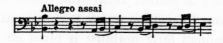

Basilio, on the other hand, speaks with legato suavity over appropriately shifty harmonies, the perfect courtier and the perfect spy:

Susanna's playful patter has now become more nervous, with good reason. The discovery of two men in her room, especially by a habitual scandalmonger, would unsettle any girl:

Strategically, Susanna faints—to a descending scale in the orchestra—but she recovers with surprising vigor as the two men try to place her in the very chair where Cherubino is hiding. A syncopated motif in the violins, to be heard again later in the trio, is a witty comment on the situation:

Basilio, oily as before, assures the Count that what he has said about Cherubino was only rumor. After his calm phrase, Susanna's *forte* outburst is proof enough that at least a part of his story is true; as Gluck commented, the violas never lie!

It is significant that the Count, in telling how he caught Cherubino once before, adopts Basilio's melody, for he has also used Basilio's tactics, spying rather than commanding. Here Mozart uses an amusing touch of instrumental color. The strings move downward with the inevitability of the Count's move toward the chair; the woodwinds are saved for the moment when he lifts the cover and finds

Mozart in a drawing made from Posch's 1789 medallion

P. A. CARON DE BEAUMARCHAIS.

Pierre Augustin Caron de Beaumarchais, whose comedy *Le Mariage de Figaro* (1784) was the basis of Mozart's opera (1786)

Lorenzo da Ponte, librettist for *The Marriage of Figaro* and first professor of Italian at Columbia University. Portrait by Samuel F. Morse, inventor of the telegraph.

Joseph II, who ordered the first performance of *The Marriage of Figaro*

Antonio Salieri, Court Conductor in Vienna, whose antagonism to Mozart hampered the first production of *The Marriage of Figaro*

The first production of Beaumarchais's *Figaro* with Molé as Almaviva, Mlle. Olivier as Cherubino, and Mlle. Contat as Susanna in the original costumes

Mozart with Maria Theresa and Joseph II in a park in Vienna

Francesco Benucci, Figaro in the première of the opera, May 1, 1786

Drawn, & Engraved by I. Condé

Mozarteum, Salzburg

Anna Salina Storace, the first Susanna, from a portrait drawn and engraved by I. Condé

Dorotea Bussani, the first
Cherubino and Despina

Michael Kelly, or O'Kelly as
he called himself in Vienna,
the first Basilio, shown at
about twenty-eight. From a
print after the portrait by
Lawrence in the collection of
Mr. Richard Northcott, Archi-
vist of the Royal Opera, Covent Garden.

Mozart at the pianoforte, 1782-1783. An unfinished oil painting from life by Joseph Lange.

Harvey Lloyd

The Mozart Monument in St. Marx's cemetery, Vienna

Cherubino; the strings quietly move upward again. Everyone, including the orchestra, is speechless with surprise. This is perhaps the funniest single moment of the first act, and Mozart plays it with the musical equivalent of a poker face. Like Susanna's appearance from the closet in Act II, it is deftly understated.

Basilio cannot conceal his delight at this little scandal, and gives a melodic giggle:

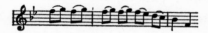

Next, pouring his own oil on the fire, he repeats his assurance that it was only a rumor. This bit of satire is Mozart's own idea, quite unplanned by the librettist but devastating in its effect on both Susanna and the Count. (Perhaps one reason for the success of the Mozart–Da Ponte combination was that the texts allowed for some imagination on the part of the composer.)

Of the ensembles with musical emphasis on action, the most obvious is the "letter duet" in Act III. Again Mozart's sense for stage timing comes to the singer's aid. Susanna is not expected to take shorthand; she has just enough time between phrases to write in a ladylike script what the Countess dictates. And what a human touch: she misses one phrase, and must ask her employer to repeat it!

Mozart rarely repeats a text without dramatic justification, and the progress of the drama usually requires some musical change in the repetition. Here the restatement of text is the most natural event possible: the secretary reads back what she has written. This time, however, no time for writing is necessary, so the phrases overlap one another closely.

A musical repetition may come about without a repetition of text, but some element of similarity in situation must be present if the form is really to illuminate the drama. In the trio of the second act, the composer has used a well-established pattern, the sonatina, which fits the dramatic pattern admirably: the exposition, or statement of two points of view, an abbreviated development preparing for the return of the first theme, and the return itself, with new consequences.

The situation is this: someone is in the Countess's closet. The Countess insists that it is Susanna; the Count, justifiably suspicious, demands in his usual imperious tone that she come out:

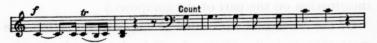

Susanna, in hiding, wonders what this is all about, while the Countess—searching for a plausible answer, over a rather uncertain chromatic accompaniment—explains that Susanna is trying on her wedding dress. This is the second theme of the sonata, the second point of view:

The preparation for the return, musically the traditional buildup of the dominant chord, brings a quick exchange of conflicting commands, the Count again ordering Susanna to come out and the Countess forbidding it. Now we arrive at the musical restatement, but with a dramatic change. The Count gives a new command: if she will not appear, she must at least speak. The Countess's reaction is uncontrolled panic:

She calls to "Susanna" to be silent. The Count, his suspicions even stronger now, ominously warns her to take care, while Susanna comments aside that only a scandal can result.

The brilliance of Susanna's part in this ensemble is curious, considering the dramatic situation. A young lady in hiding can hardly hope to remain undiscovered while running repeatedly up to high C. Mozart never intended to put her in such danger; originally the two soprano parts were reversed through most of the trio, with Susanna appropriately singing the inner voice and the Countess taking the excited runs. Some editions are still printed this way, but tradition has since assigned the lower part to the Countess's heavier voice. The composer would have been disturbed, no doubt, but Susanna retains her high C's.

The following duet, between Susanna and Cherubino, again concentrates on action. As a variety of melody was appropriate for the variety of ideas in the trio, the single purpose—escape—here calls for a single musical idea. The composer builds the entire duet on one little motif:

There is no development of the theme in a symphonic sense, but it whirls in the mind, now in one key, now in another, as the two run from door to door, find all locked, wonder what to do, and discover the convenient window. It rises in agitation as Susanna protests; it goes briefly into the minor key with charming mock-tragedy as Cherubino bids her farewell, and it ends in the air—as he jumps.

Music can give a clear indication of a psychological state, even without special aid from the text. An excellent example is the name-calling duet between Marcellina and Susanna. (I can be nicer to you than you can be to me, you hussy.) Poor Susanna, less experienced in courtly battle tactics, is on the defensive from the start. Marcellina leads; Susanna can only follow suit, repeating her melody.

Marcellina offers her double-edged compliments calmly, over a soft accompaniment; Susanna bursts out with her own in an agitated *forte*. Not until Susanna finds her weak spot—her age—does the older woman explode. Now the process begins again. The entire text is repeated, but here the two situations are reversed: Susanna is sure of herself now, Marcellina on the defensive. She attempts to change the subject, pulling away from the key of her defeat, but Susanna immediately returns to it. Marcellina offers her compliments, but Susanna is much quicker with her answers—she needs no time for thought now! Delighted with her success, she teases like a child— "Your age, your age, your age"—until her rival gives up the battle and departs, infuriated.

Again in the duet between Susanna and the Count (Act III) we hear two emotional states in contrast. The Count is lovesick, beyond any doubt. The uncertainty of A minor, a definite tension in the harmony, and a suggestion of palpitations of the heart betray him:

Susanna answers much more calmly, in the brighter C major, but obligingly modulates to the Count's key as she promises to meet him in the garden. Now the Count can relax. An expansive phrase in A major (a happy compromise of tonality) shows his confidence:

Meanwhile Susanna, in her characteristic staccato line, begs our pardon for her lie:

She is nearly caught in the lie, as Mozart again turns a text repetition to dramatic advantage: she carelessly says "no" when she means to say "yes." A sudden dissonance shows us that the Count is suspicious of the slip, but the dissonance smooths out as Susanna hastily corrects herself:

The joke is worth repeating, but the second time Mozart gives her a mistaken "yes" for variety. The Count's questions are coming so fast, by now, that even an honest witness might become confused! Susanna is a clever enough actress, however, to appear to agree with him by the end of the duet. They sing in the most convincing of parallel thirds, although their ideas are directly opposed.

It is hard to single out one predominant idea in the sextet of Act III; everything said so far applies to it in some measure. In a deliciously funny situation, the recognition of Figaro as the long-lost child of Marcellina and Bartolo, we are shown musical characterization (the two parents seen in a new and sympathetic light), relationship (the three happy characters balanced against the two disturbed ones), action (Susanna's misunderstanding and its explanation, linking her musically with first the unhappy group, then the happy one), and a most delightful instance of repetition of text for comic effect, the succession of "Sua madre?" and "Suo padre?" as Susanna incredulously questions one person after another.

Emotional state is skillfully drawn. The calmness of legato lines and harmonies firmly rooted in long pedal points for Figaro, Marcellina, and Bartolo contrasts with the abrupt phrases and angry dotted rhythms of the Count and Curzio. Susanna, seeing Figaro embrace her old rival, takes fire musically, in an agitated phrase which might be serious:

(In one of his short *Lieder*, Mozart applied the same phrase, in the same key, to another forsaken maiden, a young girl burning the letters of a faithless lover. No musical comedy here—and, as far as Susanna knows, her situation is equally hopeless.)

Marcellina explains everything, in a phrase which—curiously—bears a resemblance to her exaggerated compliments of the first act. She is still the same person, though the orchestra shows her a calmer one now:

Formally, this is the return of the opening theme, another example of the dramatic use of the sonata form. The first statement brought the son into the family; the second brings in the daughter-in-law as well. Now the reunited family's happiness contrasts with the dissatisfaction of the Count and Curzio, who break into the blissful ensemble with forceful threats and sharp changes of key:

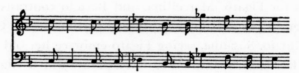

No doubt Sullivan remembered this moment when he composed *Patience:* a happy group of ladies and a disgruntled group of soldiers react in very much the same way to Mr. Bunthorne's solicitor. Sullivan could not have chosen a bettter model for the technique.

Effective in its formal design, rich in detail, always a source of added life for the drama—sometimes far beyond the actual demands of the text—the music of *Figaro* is perpetually amazing to its closest students, a delight to operagoers, and a boon to actors. No more can be said of any dramatic music. It is both beautiful and functional; it does its work excellently, and it never ceases to be music.

Mozart's Wedding Symphony

BY FREDERICK W. STERNFELD

A standard feature of *opera buffa* which Mozart and Lorenzo da Ponte incorporated into *Le Nozze di Figaro* with
consummate skill is the "finale technique," of which the
Finale to Act II serves as a shining example. Actually it is
the most extended, unified piece of music written by Mozart up to 1786. The librettist, describing his labors with
a previous work, has given us an illuminating and amusing account of a proper *buffo* finale:

> The finale, which must be closely connected with the rest
> of the opera, is a sort of little comedy in itself and requires
> a fresh plot and special interest of its own. This is the great
> occasion for showing off the genius of the composer, the
> ability of the singer and the most effective "situation" of
> the drama. Recitative is excluded from it; everything is
> sung, and every style of singing must find a place—*adagio,
> andante . . . strepitoso . . . strepitosissimo. . . .* In the finale
> it is a dogma of theatrical theology that all the singers ap-
> pear on the stage, even if there are three hundred of them,

by ones, by twos, by threes, by sixes . . . to sing solos, duets, trios, sextets. . . . If the plot of the play does not allow it, the poet must find some way . . . in defiance of his judgment, of his reason, or of all the Aristotles on earth, and if he then finds his play going badly, so much the worse for him!

Da Ponte was not one to speak modestly of himself; nevertheless he summarizes very well the difficulties of constructing a *buffo* finale. It is true: the public did expect all the singers to appear on the stage—and so, for that matter, did the singers—to insure their proper share of the applause. In weak librettos this routine has a mechanical quality that reminds one of a puppet show. But Da Ponte, that remarkable man, constructs "a little comedy in itself" for the Act II Finale of *Figaro,* where the entrances of the characters seem to be the result of dramatic necessity and cumulatively produce "the most effective situation of the drama."

To begin with, the Count, who suspects Cherubino, argues with the Countess (Section 1):

The closet is finally opened; instead of the expected Cherubino there emerges, to the Count's stupefaction and embarrassment, Susanna (Section 2, *andante,* triple time). We now have three characters or, musically speaking, three voices. The Count asks his wife to forgive him (Section 3, *allegro,* duple time). So far, so good. But these dramatic scaffoldings must also serve as the "occasion for showing off the genius of the composer." By analogy with the writing of the *Entführung* libretto we may assume that Mozart made suggestions to Da Ponte which guided the librettist in offering such opportunities. One was the surprise when Susanna emerges from the closet: such a denouement invariably provoked Mozart to write with true dramatic insight, avoiding obvious clichés. The usual formula in eighteenth-century opera (as well as twentieth-century films) was to accompany dramatic disclosures with great fanfare. But consider the normal reaction of a human being when faced with the unexpected: we are mute, or merely whisper, unable to muster our strength, and we stammer as if to gain time and poise.

Mozart's "quiet" climaxes are justly famed for their uncanny portrayal of a human response. One instance occurs in the first act of *Figaro* (Trio No. 7), when the Count discovers Cherubino poised on the arm of Susanna's chair, and another in the Finale of Act I in *Don Giovanni,* when Masetto is discovered in the bushes. But the surprise in the *Figaro* Act II Finale has a special, soulful poignancy. Not only is the Count suddenly confronted by Susanna instead of Cherubino, which would be plain comedy, but also by the object of his advances, and painfully he realizes that this fact is not unknown to the Countess. Quickly, quietly, the little orchestral figure repeats itself, finally coming

to a halt as if it had run out of strength and breath (last
bars of Section 1). Then again, quietly but ironically,
Susanna challenges the Count in triple time—that is, in
music that is really a slow minuet, the aristocratic measure
in which the lower-born are wont to mock the aristocracy
(see Figaro's "Se vuol ballare"):

Susanna's slow and soft minuet (Section 2) is then
succeeded by a typical *buffo* trio (Section 3) in which the
women first scold the Count and then give in to his pleading. Once more Mozart's genius intervenes: instead of the
conventional bubbling we are touched by a passage where
the three voices are united in simple homophony (the
words are *Da questo momento*), and the soft chords of the
wind instruments mysteriously suggest the peace to be
achieved at the conclusion of the opera:

These first three sections of the Finale are, in effect,
equivalent to the first movement of a sonata or a concerto.
Since "recitative is excluded" from the *buffo* finale and, as
Da Ponte puts it, everything is sung, Mozart took advantage of the occasion to make of that little comedy a unified
piece of music, not a mere succession of vocal numbers.
The following two portions of the Finale (Section 4, *allegro*, triple time; Section 5, *andante*, duple time) introduce another singer, Figaro. The contrast to the earlier
sections suggests the middle movements of a symphony.
The *allegro*, at which point Figaro enters, clearly has the
function of a scherzo, whereas the calming *andante* which
succeeds it is full of the emotional intensity of a slow
movement. In this fifth section Mozart gives us another
of those mysterious passages where an exquisite beauty
touches the heart. The Italian words are *Deh signor, nol
contrastate;* as in the earlier passage (*Da questo momento*
in Section 3), the voices enter softly, *sotto voce,* over a pedal
point:

Deh si - gnor, nol con - tra - sta - te, con - so - la - tei miei de - sir,

This time the texture of the music is more polyphonic,
and so persuasive is the pleading of Figaro, Susanna, and
the Countess that even the Count, though intriguing
against them, sings to their melody as he quietly wishes
for Marcellina, Basilio, and Bartolo to appear. It is an in-

stance where the public receives more than it expects, for within the conventional finale of comic opera we have a beauty that eclipses, though by no means obliterates, the supporting structure. Ultimately, his idealism and seriousness of purpose thwarted Mozart's success with his public, which was neither accustomed to nor prepared for such depth in Italian *opera buffa*. But *Figaro* is still this side of the line: the expansion comes as a wonderful surprise, but the familiar structure is never distorted beyond recognition.

The Finale is now rounded off by its final portions (Section 6, *allegro,* duple time; Section 7, *andante,* modified triple time; Section 8, *allegro,* duple time), which correspond to the first three sections much the way the last movement of a symphony corresponds to the first. Four additional singers make their appearance, first Antonio and later the trio of intriguers—Marcellina, Bartolo, Basilio— who threaten to put an end to the marriage of Figaro and Susanna once and for all:

Allegro assai

Voi,   si - gnor,   che giu - sto   sie-te,

This continuous, unified composition of Mozart's, as long as an entire symphony, paved the way for his great successor, Beethoven. The novel structure of Beethoven's Fifth Symphony, which lasts nearly half an hour, and the Ninth, almost an hour in length, would be difficult to conceive without the achievement of Mozart's *buffo* finales, particularly the one which, occurring at the very center of *Le Nozze di Figaro,* constitutes both the heart of the music and the fulcrum of the action.

Marriages in *Figaro*

BY JOSEPH KERMAN

During the Finale to the fourth act of *The Marriage of Figaro,* the plot becomes more and more complicated. In and out of the rococo summerhouses, shaded even from the starlight, the masters and servants make love, mistake one another, and invariably discover Cherubino when they least want him around. Count Almaviva tries to seduce his own wife, who is disguised as Susanna, and Figaro pretends to make love to the Countess (actually his Susanna in disguise). Things come to a head when the Count overhears this last maneuver; alas, he is without his sword; he summons torches and prepares a scene of public humiliation for the faithless wife. She (Susanna in disguise, that is) acts out a frantic plea for mercy, as do Figaro and the entire court; the Count is adamant, until the real Countess enters and throws aside Susanna's clothes: "Perhaps my entreaties may prevail." Suddenly all the busy gaiety is gone from the music. There is an abrupt turn to the minor

mode, a hush, a tense new rhythm, and a nervous har-
monic progression to portray the general stupefaction and
the desperate confusion of the Count.* This brief section
changes the mood drastically, and prepares for an even
greater change as the Count contritely begs and gains forgiveness from the Countess. *Andante* now, for the moment, and an altogether unexpected, unprecedented still-
ness and simplicity:

It is a climax on every level. On the level of the intrigue,
it forms the denouement; but the plane of the drama is
gently lifted far above the evening's escapades. On the
level of the personalities, the Count shows an unsuspected
capacity for humility, and none of the breast-beating that
marked the mock pleas of Figaro and Susanna, a minute
before; the Countess has never been more lovely and true
to herself; even the Basilios and Cherubinos are touched.
On the most profound level of all, the scene uncovers a
core of decency under all the shabbiness which the farce
has exposed and tried to rationalize in laughter. All this
is possible because *musically* it is a climax, because the
music now has a deeper seriousness, a sublimity and a

* A year later, Mozart used very similar musical means at another critical
unmasking: in *Don Giovanni,* when Donna Anna and her friends capture
Leporello disguised as Giovanni.

new clarity of feeling. Mozart here foreshadows his vision
in *The Magic Flute.*

Unquestionably he meant this reconciliation to be the
greatest moment in the opera, and certainly he knew his
business well enough to make us feel it, too. If this is the
greatest moment in *Figaro*, all our understanding of the
drama must work backward from it. The effect is entirely
Mozart's, by the way; neither Beaumarchais's original play
nor Da Ponte's libretto gives any inkling of the force of
the scene in the opera. Here is a fairly literal translation
of the libretto at this point:

COUNT: Forgive me, Countess.
COUNTESS: I am more gentle, And answer you "yes."
ALL: We all are delighted
           To have it end thus!

That is all. With this miserable material before him,
where did Mozart get the idea for the sudden revelation
that he chose to build around it, for the meeting of husband and wife on terms that we had never dreamed were
still available to them? And yet, does their reconciliation
really come as such a surprise?

On the contrary, the scene has been very carefully prepared. The Count and Countess, of course, have always
been serious people, well aware of their incongruity with
everyone around them: Figaro, Susanna, Bartolo, Marcellina, Basilio, Antonio, and Barbarina all wear the stock
masks of the *commedia dell'arte* (though the personality
peeps out from behind the *persona*). Perhaps the Countess

rather tends to dramatize her plight, in "Porgi, amor" and "Dove sono," but Mozart sees to it that we believe and trust in her; there is no melodrama at the end. But also, at the end, we cannot help recalling another reconciliation, earlier in the piece, when Figaro is discovered to be the long-lost son of Don Bartolo and Marcellina, who happily get married, at last, and forget all about the marriage contract between Figaro and Marcellina. Thanks to Beaumarchais, it is a hilarious moment; thanks to Mozart, it is also a strangely beautiful one. Unreliable tradition reports that of all the numbers in the opera, the sextet here was Mozart's favorite. The touching, comic ecstasy of the two old people at finding their "little Raffaello" is set off against the exasperation of the Count (foiled *again!*); and in the last section of the piece, warm harmonies suggest a serenity in human relationships which had not been indicated before. Of course, Bartolo and Marcellina as characters are lightly sketched; but Mozart could not resist humanizing Beaumarchais's puppets whenever he could, especially when he had a good reason. The main point is that he wanted to give a strong hint, as early as this, of salvation even for such sadly separated people as the Count and Countess.

The sextet also opens up a significant subplot by showing the first signs of friction in the glib little love nest of Figaro and Susanna: when she sees him embracing Marcellina (*sua madre?*) she flares up and boxes his ears. This theme is developed in the last act, especially in the Finale.

Figaro thinks that Susanna is really flirting with the
Count; he sings a sardonic aria about infidelity, "Aprite
un po' quegl'occhi." She thinks that he is really courting
the Countess; in her best *commedia dell'arte* fashion, she
slaps him some more. They settle their differences just before the Count and Countess do.

At first, one might regard this subplot as an obvious
device to produce additional comic situations. It is, but
it is also more: it becomes a genuine dramatic element by
setting up a manifest analogy between Figaro and Susanna
on the one hand and the Count and Countess on the other.
Susanna sings "Deh vieni," and confirms Figaro's worst
fears by her ambiguous phraseology, not so much because
she wants to make him jealous but because Mozart did;
the dramaturgy may be a little clumsy here, but the purpose it serves is important. Mozart loved dramatic paral-
lels of this kind. In the *Seraglio* he has Belmonte-Constanz
versus Pedrillo-Blonde, in *Così Fan Tutte* Ferrando-Fior-
diligi versus Guglielmo-Dorabella, in *The Magic Flute*
(most explicitly of all) Tamino-Pamina versus Papageno-
Papagena. In every case the pairs complement each other
carefully, and in *Figaro* the analogy is hammered home
by having the two women actually pose as one another.

To contrast Figaro-Susanna and the Count-Countess
in the complex matters of love, desertion, jealousy, suspicion, and forgiveness is very revealing and of great importance to Mozart's conception. With the servants, the
causes for jealousy are only imaginary. Their feelings are

more or less trivial: Susanna slaps Figaro, and he *generalizes* his anger at her betrayal into a diatribe against women in general. Their reconciliation is correspondingly superficial: they are safely hidden behind their *commedia dell' arte* masks in the charming duet where all is forgiven:

pa - ce, mio te - ne - ro a - mor!

pa - ce, mio te - ne - ro a - mor!

Operatic people who sing in thirds and sixths are never very genuine. Compare the situation with the Count and Countess. There has been cause for jealousy here, on the other side; the Count has a regular squad of panderers. But instead of jealousy the Countess expresses her poignant grief. His fury when his schemes are thwarted, or when he thinks her unfaithful, is intense and highly unpleasant: as has frequently been observed, Almaviva is Mozart's most savage creation. Yet in spite of injury and high feelings, their reconciliation is deep and true, the most beautiful thing in the opera. The doors of Wisdom, Love, and Virtue are not far away.

Beaumarchais's play had "social significance" in its time, and Mozart's opera too, we are told, sets forth a cunning criticism of the *ancien régime* in its exaltation of the honest lower classes. I cannot see it that way. For Mozart, as for Shakespeare with *King* Lear and *Prince* Hamlet, nobility of station is the clear symbol for nobility of spirit.

The court may smirk, but the Count and Countess have interested us more profoundly than any of the court intrigues. She is not strong, he is not good, and even their servants can show them up as pathetic and ludicrous. But they are *conscious,* they feel their feelings through, and there is a ground of sympathy between them which Figaro and Susanna cannot ever comprehend. Cruelty and shame have their place in Mozart's picture of human fallibility; particularly in this context, his ending reveals a view of life that is realistic, unsentimental, optimistic, and humane. Probably no one has left a performance of *Figaro* without thinking, well, the Count will soon be philandering again. But just as surely there will be another reconciliation, another renewal as genuine, as contrite, and as beautiful as the one that still moves us as we leave the theater. Are clever Figaro and shallow Susanna actually so secure?

Opera for Mozart was more than musical comedy, and his operas survive not because they are full of pretty tunes, but because they disclose or organize for us something about the business of living. And this is done by the music; on the essential level, it is music that articulates the reconciliation of *Figaro* and everything that has led up to it. The insight is Mozart's, and so are the dramatic means that can convey it to an audience two centuries removed.

Master of Human Insight

BY TIBOR KOZMA

Beaumarchais's *Mariage de Figaro* is credited with—or accused of—having helped precipitate the French Revolution. No effects quite so spectacular and drastic have ever been ascribed to the opera based on Beaumarchais's fist-clenching comedy, Mozart's *Le Nozze di Figaro*. On the surface, it looks as though Mozart had summed up and developed great trends that had been in existence before him rather than blazed new trails. Indeed, his operas would have been hardly thinkable without the influence of Pergolesi, Handel, and Gluck. It is not so much Mozart's originality—a quality very much overrated by the esthetics of the individualistic nineteenth century—that made him the greatest of all operatic composers. It was rather his entirely new attitude, his *modern* personal concept of this form of art, as we see it, that became the most decisive influence on operatic history up to our own twentieth century, up to Richard Strauss's *Rosenkavalier*.

45

We hold this true in spite of the fact that there meanwhile occurred in the field of opera the atomic explosion that was Richard Wagner, a phenomenon which temporarily blinded many eyes and deafened many ears to the different kind of greatness in Mozart.

We could hardly hope to understand Mozart's relationship to the artistic problem of opera without pointing out one of the most significant traits of his personality. In his subjective experience, in his personal contact with the world, in trying to protect his most vital interests or guard himself against lies and intrigues, Mozart showed a bewildering and pathetic helplessness throughout his life in the judgment of other people's characters. However, as soon as personally disinterested, objective, naïve, purely artistic observation entered into play, there appeared in him—from his earliest childhood—a downright uncanny sureness, a clairvoyant penetration of the innermost and most secret recesses of the human soul, with an almost magically unerring instinct for psychological understanding that is far ahead of his entire epoch. Almost every one of his letters is witness to this perplexing contradiction which, in a musician of his caliber, was bound to direct an important portion of his creative energies toward the musical stage.

This instinctive wisdom—or wisdom of instincts—determined Mozart's whole approach to opera. It made him place the *human being,* the ordinary, everyday human being, in the center of interest. While Gluck, the greatest musical dramatist before Mozart, dealt with the primordial emotions—love, hatred, vengeance, passion—in terms of stylized, over-life-size heroes and heroines inspired by the Greek tragedy; while Wagner, with the sole exception of *Die Meistersinger von Nürnberg*, sought to explore philosophical problems of universal validity in his music dramas, Mozart's hero is, to use twentieth-century parlance, the common man. There are no perfect, flawless, uncontradictory characters on Mozart's stage, there are no completely black villains and no entirely blameless heroes, only people of our own kind who may wear very different clothes but whose strong and weak, good and evil qualities we have often encountered in our own lives.

The philandering Count Almaviva, for example, is anything but an attractive personality. From his first appearance, the music describes him as a choleric, petty tyrant; loud, rough, trampling, ostentatious chords in the orchestra and brusque accents in the vocal part accompany him wherever he goes; in his third-act aria he reveals himself, to the pompous sounds of trumpets and timpani, as a fellow who is just as ready to take revenge for being offended as he is to offend others. And yet this selfsame Almaviva, with all his raving and ranting, with all the display of his unabashed sensuousness, makes us smile too often at the humorous and somewhat embarrassing situations into which he keeps getting himself to think of him as completely hateful. And it is this same Count who seems to find his better self in one of the most wonderful phrases of

the Finale ("Contessa, perdono!"), a phrase which marks
a turning point in the turbulent happenings and leads up
to a real apotheosis of all that is good and decent in
human hearts and of all that is beautiful in Mozart's
music.

Perhaps "the villain of the piece" is no real villain at all
but merely a blundering, perhaps not always very agree-
able, yet quite understandable specimen of the male animal. How does Mozart see his dramatic counterpart, the
long-suffering Countess? Certainly, she is the nearest thing
to what Gottfried Keller called "The loveliest of poet's
vices: to invent sweet women's images which cannot be
found on this bitter earth." The very first bars of the
second act with which she is introduced bring an entirely
new color and a new atmosphere of purity, warmth, and
womanly grace, high above the sphere of intrigues in
which the plot had moved so far. Her third-act aria "Dove
sono . . . ," christened "Dove Song" by some insipid pun-
ster, has always reminded this listener of the cool, chaste,
marble grandeur of Gluck. Yet, we also see this great lady
receiving the adoration of the young and angelically handsome Cherubino (a future Almaviva in cocoon!) with no
displeasure at all. We see her participating in all the in-
volved cabals of the opera just enough to realize that she
is also human and not too closely related to all the incredibly noble and incredibly heroic young ladies who—
now in blond, now in black wigs—populate a great deal

of the non-Mozartian stage, seldom remaining alive until the finale.

As a last example watch Marcellina, when she first appears, as near to the typical half-ridiculous, half-repulsive old woman as was ever exploited on the comedy stage through the centuries. Yet, once her warped life regains its sane perspective, through the discovery of her long-lost son Figaro and the attainment of respectability as Bartolo's spouse-to-be, this same Marcellina sings some of the loveliest, most warmhearted music of the entire score, in the third-act sextet. Here, too, Mozart's psychology penetrates deeply and does not allow one of the drama's persons to degenerate into a mere cliché.

Wherever we look, we find the same unfailing power of this music in portraying that incredibly complicated, never entirely good or bad, never entirely attractive or repulsive, never entirely positive or negative phenomenon called the human being. Mozart is the very focus, the concentration, of all the attempts to present, to explore, to explain this phenomenon on the musical-dramatic stage. Perhaps Wagner went beyond him in the grandeur of his concept; perhaps the elemental power of Verdi's dramatic ideas gets closer at times to Shakespeare's naïve truth; but never, in all operatic history, were people observed with such keen understanding or projected onto the scene with such vitality as in the dramatic works of Mozart.

Meet Marcellina

BY ANN M. LINGG

First of all, Marcellina is not identical with Berta, Dr. Bartolo's maid in *The Barber*. Her full name is Marceline de Verte-Allure, and she starts out as the mystery woman of Beaumarchais's play, confined to her room with a sore foot contracted as a result of Figaro's medical ministrations. She is Rosina's ex-governess and looks after Bartolo's household; about thirty years ago she was his mistress and bore him a son, who has mysteriously disappeared. Shocked into virtue, she now wears somber clothes and whiles away many an evening with a good book. As a result, she has developed sophistication and both moral and intellectual pride; the pert little Susanna, whom Rosina hires after marrying the Count, is a thorn in her side.

Marcellina is about fifty years old and still attractive to men—quite eligible, in fact, in the eyes of Don Basilio. He, too, went to live in the Almaviva castle, where he pursues her with his love. This is music to the ears of

Bartolo, who is haunted by fear of having to marry her himself, yet who relishes even more the prospect of marrying her off to Figaro, with whom he has scores to settle.

Exactly when Marcellina discovers her passionate affinity for Susanna's "handsome, amiable, gay" fiancé is left to our imagination. Da Ponte's libretto introduces her to us fully enamored, and ready to blackmail Figaro into matrimony by fair means or foul. She suffers agonies as Susanna, twittering cheerfully, proceeds with marriage preparations. At the height of her distress, on the morning of the wedding day, she sends for her former lover, who is still living in Seville; she has not seen him since moving out of his house. Sputtering and haughty, without even knocking at the door (which, incidentally, is a nicety conspicuously absent in Almaviva's household), the pair burst into Susanna's future abode. The parchment that Marcellina waves furiously in her hands is the crucial prop: Figaro's promissory note that he will either raise the 10,000 francs he owes her or make her his wife.

After swearing vengeance, Bartolo stalks off. Marcellina, sure of her superiority, decides to scare Susanna and cut her down to infinitesimal size with allusions to gossip. The brief duet between the two women is really a verbal duel, a competition in cattiness. First Marcellina has the upper hand, infuriating Susanna with pointed sarcasm. Susanna fumbles angrily for rejoinders until she has the inspiration to mention their difference in age. She laughs in triumph as Marcellina loses ground. It's all in the music; the in-

sults of the two women come hard and fast, almost inter-
rupting each other until a few bars of orchestral postlude
find Marcellina literally speechless, and she rushes out,
bristling with rage.

Backstage, she grabs Bartolo by the hand and insists
that he go with her to Seville to see a lawyer. As Cherubino makes sure that complications will not stop piling
up, the pair race into town and back in time for the second-
act Finale.

There is a temptation to make Marcellina all crude
comedy, old and foolish. To be sure, there is a strong element of farce in the aging matron who wants to marry
her own son until she recognizes him by a birthmark; but
in the third-act recognition scene, Marcellina becomes so
genuinely human, so feeling and moving, that to have
parodied her too strongly would make the transformation
implausible.

The poor woman is happy for the first time in her life!
A moment ago she was scorned, rejected by everybody
except the repulsive Basilio; now suddenly she has a husband and a grown-up son, even a daughter. Her about-face
toward Susanna is sudden and complete. Beaumarchais
makes her apologize to Figaro for her nasty behavior toward his bride, and in the play's fourth act, when she finds
him jealous and despondent, she has a few wise things to say
about marriage. Da Ponte, who had great trouble at this
point condensing the play to keep the action going and
give every soloist a musical chance, traded advice for an

aria—usually omitted as superfluous to an already long opera. Here Mozart wrote cheerful music for her, giving her long coloraturas that she might not have been able to sing a few hours before, when she burst into Susanna's room like a goddess of vengeance. In the large company of pathetic, lovelorn mezzos, Marcellina holds a special place: she grows younger by the minute!

And she held a special place for Beaumarchais, who retroactively gave her a mission after his play was performed. Confronted by indignant reviewers, Marcellina became a standard-bearer of his philosophy of virtue. The critics resented being obliged to discuss an immoral woman, feeling that Marcellina, far from being overjoyed at finding her lost son, should consider herself "punished for her shame." Such hypocritical nonsense Beaumarchais countered with a priceless twist. He had invented this humiliated creature, he said, to draw public attention to the real culprits in such situations: men who seduce young women.

"The man who judges us here today has in his time caused the downfall of perhaps ten unhappy girls!" exclaims Beaumarchais's Marceline passionately. "You, and you alone, should be punished for the errors of our youth!" And in his preface to *Le Mariage de Figaro,* the author adds wistfully that he considers the corruption of young girls the thing most destructive of public virtue, holding up Marceline as an example that his play was censored only because he was right.

Mooncalves

BY MARY WATKINS CUSHING

Once upon a time, a certain celebrated and expensive prima donna rejected the beautiful role of the Marschallin in an important premiere of Strauss's *Der Rosenkavalier* out of simple pique that another soprano had been chosen for Octavian. She lived, presumably, to regret it, but this rash and foolish decision points up a curious fact in the lore of the music theater: the attraction for the female, quite regardless of her personal size and shape, of an opportunity to strut about in doublet and hose. Composers and librettists have long recognized this craving and from time to time have graciously, or sometimes maliciously, included in their cast of characters a beardless boy. These youths scamper or languish through the pages of many famous scores, promoting or delaying the action as the plot requires, and the most irresistible of them all—with due respect to Octavian—is Cherubino in "The Marriage of Figaro."

He is the mooncalf par excellence. Not only has he two

delightful little arias to sing, with the center of the stage all his ("Non so più cosa son" in Act I and "Voi che sapete" in Act II), but the presentation of the boy's character, musically and dramatically, shines with pure creative genius. He has all the qualities that the nicest, most maddening adolescent can hope to possess. He is mischievous, shy and bold at once, clumsy, ardent, sentimental, alternately playful and enormously earnest, romantic to absurdity. His everyday affair with young Barbarina is as touching in its way as the suffocating pangs of adoration that he professes so boyishly for the Countess.

Cherubino is a role no singer need despise, even though it ranks a technical third in the cast. Its requirements—not always met—are a fresh, clear soprano or mezzo voice, at least an approximation of youth and high spirits, bright features, lean flanks and a delicate sense of fun. There have been some very famous Cherubinos; in 1909 none other than Geraldine Farrar joined a cast such as has never been heard since, with Eames as the Countess, Marcella Sembrich as Susanna, Adamo Didur as Figaro, and Antonio Scotti as Almaviva. Did the gilded audiences in those days appreciate this largesse? Perhaps they did, but it is a safe and sad assumption that Sembrich's lovely but late aria, "Deh! vieni," drifted over rapidly emptying boxes, and that Cherubino's final exuberances were played to a fashionably departing throng. Such was the fate of last acts in the mauve decade.

For Octavian, the romantic young Graf Rofrano of

Rosenkavalier, we fortunately encounter a more respectful public in which almost no one seems willing to forego the enchantment of the final trio and duet of women's voices. Octavian is a role considered virtually surefire for any soprano not too plump who has mezzo tones in her range, or vice versa. He mixes, like Cherubino, the charm of boyish ardor with prankishness, and although his relations with the Marschallin may seem somewhat preposterous, one has only to witness (as did this writer long ago in Budapest) a performance of the role by a tenor to realize that Strauss knew what he was doing when he prescribed a woman.

Another plum for mooncalves is Siébel in *Faust,* a sort of amiable nuisance in Marguerite's life. His role is brief enough, but at least he has the stage all to himself for his (unfortunately hackneyed) Flower Song, "Faites-lui mes aveux," addressing the blossoms for his lady, which he has thriftily picked from her own garden. There never seems to have been any trouble casting this comparatively small and sentimental role. The famous Scalchi sang it first at the early Metropolitan. In 1886, before *Faust* had been given so often that the Opera House was called the "Faust-spielhaus," Siébel became the property of the equally renowned Marianne Brandt.

Reverting to so-called nuisances, we have one prime example of the breed among our mooncalves, the ubiquitous and irritating Frederick in *Mignon,* an opera that is chronically out of the repertory but has always been popular. One might say that such popularity is in spite of, not because of, Frederick, one of those bumptious individuals who always appear on the scene uninvited. This young popinjay struts about wherever he has no business to be and generally blusters and brags *ad nauseam*. But the first New York Frederick was none other than Sofia Scalchi, sung to the Mignon of Christine Nilsson in 1883 and apparently much applauded. Scalchi also sang the first Metropolitan Urbain in *Les Huguenots* in 1884. This is a part not essentially a mooncalf, although his attentions to Queen Marguerite are very affecting: Urbain is a page who likes to meddle in affairs above his station.

Another page, Oscar in *A Masked Ball,* was once the property of Hempel and Alten and is considered a prize among operatic boys. Although not enamored of anyone in particular—unless, from a distance, Amelia or the witch, Ulrica, whom he promotes so enthusiastically—he plays a small but important part in the questionable proceedings of the plot.

The roster of operatic ladies masquerading as males may be much longer than the present catalogue. Mignon herself, for instance, assumes temporarily the uniform of her lover's page, and Gilda steps into tights and cloak on one desperate occasion while Beethoven's Fidelio is a famous impersonation, scarely in the same category; but these are disguises rather than impersonations. The blushing boys are rarer; some of them are expendable today and some are immortal. Cherubino and Octavian will never grow old or be unloved—nor, for that matter, will their creators or even their admirers.

The Clarinet in *Figaro*

BY TIBOR KOZMA

Among the instruments that we have come to regard as
necessary and meaningful (the word "indispensable"
should not be employed too liberally) in our orchestra, the
clarinet is the youngest. It is "only" about 250 years old,
a mere baby if we think of the flutes of the Egyptians, the
primitive organ of Ctesibius, King David's harp, the
Arabic shawms, or, last but not least, the prehistoric horns.

The inventor of the clarinet was actually a kind of cross-
breeder. Johann Christoph Denner—the man credited with
having built the first clarinet—already knew the modern-
ized shawm that the French called *hautbois,* and his in-
novation was essentially the construction of a new kind of
mouthpiece, combining some features of the oboe's double
reed with the beak of the recorder and some ideas of his
own. The result was that beaklike mouthpiece with a
single reed, larger than that of the oboe, which we see today on our clarinets and also on that offspring of a later

crossbreeding: the saxophone. The recorder also influenced Denner inasmuch as he built his new instrument in cylindrical form rather than in the conical shape of the oboe. However, the determining factor for a wind instrument's musical color is its mouthpiece; the rest is up to practical, mechanical, and technical considerations, important to the performer rather than to the music-loving listener for whom this is written.

Oboe and clarinet, then, are very close relatives but also quite different musical personalities. The former is the ingénue, the latter the emotional heroine; the oboe is the soubrette, the clarinet the lyric-dramatic soprano or even mezzo-soprano. In both tonal and dynamic range, the clarinet is the most versatile member of the woodwind family, especially since today it is built in vastly differing sizes, from the high and squeaky E-flat instrument down to the hauntingly melancholy, romantic bass clarinet. We encounter most frequently the clarinets in A or B-flat, instruments capable of playing within the compass of more than three octaves, capable also of the most tender *pianissimo* effects, rivaled in this respect only by the flute which, however, never possesses the clarinet's emotional intensity. Their tonal fullness can well hold its own against an entire orchestra.

The first occurrence of the clarinet in art music is found in one of Rameau's operas, about 1750. From France it traveled to Mannheim, the eighteenth-century capital of symphonic music, and there it was discovered by the young

Mozart, who wrote about it with great enthusiasm in a letter to his father. Nevertheless, even Mozart employed it only sporadically; at the height of his creative strength, he orchestrated his great G minor Symphony first without clarinets and added them only later. To this very day, the discussion whether the symphony should be performed with or without clarinets is by no means concluded. In his last, perhaps greatest symphonic work, the "Jupiter" Symphony, he dispensed with them altogether. It remained for Beethoven to incorporate the clarinet permanently into the symphony orchestra.

There is hardly anything in Mozart's operas that illuminates his dramatic genius more strikingly than his handling of the orchestra. In *Figaro,* and of course in *Don Giovanni, Così Fan Tutte, The Abduction from the Seraglio,* and *The Magic Flute* as well, one might say that a different kind of orchestra and orchestration is used in every number. The psychological keenness of the dramatic instinct that makes Mozart decide when to use, and, just as often, when *not* to use, a certain coloristic factor has never been excelled even by the great magicians of orchestration, Wagner, Strauss, or Puccini.

The overture to *Figaro* is scored for the entire orchestra, comprising two flutes, two oboes, two clarinets, two bassoons, two horns, two trumpets, two timpani, and strings. The clarinets are heard for one brief moment when, after the shadowy hurry of the first unison bars, a little descending phrase of oboes and horns is answered by an ascending motif of flutes and clarinets, but, on the whole, the latter are only called upon to add body to *tutti* passages and do not obtain soloistic prominence. Roughly speaking, Mozart might have written the overture entirely without clarinets and we would never know the difference.

After the overture, Mozart dismisses the trumpets, the timpani, and the clarinets for some time and opens the proceedings with an orchestra composed of the ever-present strings, flutes, oboes, bassoons, and horns, a combination that is just right for the playful happiness of the first two duets between Figaro and Susanna. Trumpets and timpani would be too aggressive for this music—and as to the clarinets? Well, we shall see. Figaro's defiant "Se vuol ballare" dispenses, characteristically enough, even with the flutes, whose voice could only detract from the sharpness of the horns that really give this number its punch. Bartolo's pompous, grandiloquent buffo aria *must* mobilize the trumpets and the timpani, while the following—shall we say, somewhat feline—duet between Susanna and Marcellina returns us to the standard instrumentation of the beginning. Still no clarinets! By now we might begin to wonder whether Mozart did not quite know what to do with them—or, perhaps, is he saving them for some very special moment?

The answer comes with the sixth number and the emergence of a new figure in the play. Cherubino is not only a new figure in this play but, indeed, a new factor in both realism and poetry of characterization which was to

haunt the world of opera up to our own epoch. To introduce Cherubino and to set him apart from the emotional
level of what has taken place thus far, Mozart resorts to three
incredibly simple devices. An excited, panting, declama-
tory line of the voice replaces the cantilena; a flowing,
waving, legato orchestral fabric appears in place of the
precise, pulsating crispness of the previous numbers; and
the clarinets take the lead in the accompaniment. So emphatic is Mozart about this new color that he actually dispenses with flutes and oboes lest their kindred voices,
moving in a similar range, overshadow the blushing,
languishing, restrained sensuousness of the clarinets. Sup-
ported by the lower and less shiny bassoons, the clarinets
are the dominant obbligato instruments throughout Cherubino's aria, punctuating his words with softly insistent
syncopations, coloring the music with sustained long notes,
singing and sighing in unison with his words, or accom-
panying them (. . . *che il suon de'vani accenti portano via
con se*) in soft thirds.

In the following agitated trio, the clarinets remain in
the orchestra to give color to Basilio's sanctimoniousness
(*Ah, già svien la poverina* and the parallel phrase *Siamo
qui per aiutarvi*). Thereafter they disappear for the rest
of the first act. Even the massive "military" music in
Figaro's "Non più andrai," drawing upon the strength of
trumpets and timpani, is scored for the entire orchestra
minus the clarinets. Again, Mozart "saves" them for an
important dramatic moment: the introduction of the
Countess.

Like Cherubino, the Countess is not merely a new
figure among the dramatis personae. Her first appearance
means an altogether new and different atmosphere, a different emotional level. There are no flutes or oboes, of
course no trumpets or timpani, in her first aria; only the
warmest colors—clarinets, bassoons, horns—are employed
in this poetic music, weaving a luminous halo of sound
around the immaculate beauty of the soprano's melody.

Cherubino's ensuing arietta again features a totally different kind of orchestration. Hitherto, the woodwinds—
with some occasional exception of the flute—have always
appeared in pairs; now they become highly individualistic
solo instruments. Only *one* flute, *one* oboe, *one* clarinet,
and *one* bassoon are combined with two horns and the
strings, with the latter playing pizzicato throughout the
number, acting as a great guitar to accompany the voice.
The solo clarinet is heard at the beginning, anticipating
Cherubino's melody by way of introduction. Especially
charming and characteristic is the role of the instrumental
soloists when (at the words *Donne vedete s'io l'ho nel cor*)
the longing, chromatically ascending motif of the clarinet
is answered by the rococo grace and playfulness of the flute
and the oboe.

There is not space within the compass of this book to
point out every instance in this marvelous score in
which the clarinet's musical personality and Mozart's uncanny ability always to find the *mot juste* in terms of coloristic expression can be observed to best advantage. Still,
the temptation cannot be resisted to point out one moment

in the last Finale when, after the exit of the Count and the (disguised) Countess, Figaro sings *Tutto tranquillo e placido,* and the music, taking its cue from these words rather than from the excitement of the situation, affords us a little breathing spell by singing out in a wonderful short nocturnal *larghetto,* with the clarinets (appearing for the first time in the Finale) and the horns casting a soft glow of soothing warmth over the scene of intrigue and agitation, reminding us that all this torment and confusion are only a passing moment in the world of beauty and happiness that Mozart's genius created.

The Court Jester

BY ROBERT BREUER

Much of the massive output of Johannes Scherr (1817–86), a Swabian-born pamphleteer and philosophical analyst of society past and present, lies buried in the maelstrom of naturalism and realism that has overtaken European and American literature in the twentieth century. Scherr should be revisited, however, if only for his *Human Tragicomedy*, a four-volume work dealing with individuals whose foibles or fancies changed history. A man who combined great vivacity of style with sharp sarcasm and occasional bluntness, Scherr was concerned with showing how one generation could profit from the mistakes of another.

Among sixty-odd chapters of the *Tragicomedy*—dealing with dictators, dreamers, witches, rebels, visionaries, and charlatans often in the guise of kings, statesmen, generals, priests, and courtesans—it is not surprising to find an incisive portrait of one Pierre Augustin Caron, who disliked the plebeian sound of his name and decided to write under a nom de plume, "de Beaumarchais." Caron-Beaumarchais—rebellious, quixotic, brilliant—was just the type to intrigue Scherr, who traced his career with care.

Beaumarchais, in addition to his playwriting, was a courtier, litigant, spy, publisher, and pamphleteer. A self-made man, he was the son of a watchmaker, but though he doffed the name Caron, he never denied his humble origin. In fact, it was his skill in the family trade that first won him public recognition. At twenty Caron had invented an important new gadget for regulating watches, the escapement. A rival watchmaker, one Lepaute, appropriated the honor of the invention; Caron, angered by the injustice, fought relentlessly until he had brought the whole matter before the court of the Academy of Sciences. His eloquent plea, a masterpiece of oratory, not only won his suit but attracted the attention of the King, who later made use of Beaumarchais's active brain in a confidential capacity.

It was Beaumarchais's intimate knowledge of the corrupt court of the Louis' which enabled him to write his pointed satires, *The Barber of Seville* and *The Marriage of Figaro*. Because he poked fun at the aristocrats, there were difficulties in obtaining royal permission for the plays to be performed. Scherr recalls the dramatic scene when a certain Mme. Campan read the manuscript *Figaro* to Louis XVI and Marie Antoinette. When Mme. Campan reached the climax of the gay comedy, Figaro's famous monologue

(Act V)—the war cry of an enslaved, suffering people against the frivolous aristocracy—the King interrupted her, shouting angrily, "This is horrible. Never will this dangerous comedy be performed on the stage! Who knows what the consequences would be? This man pokes fun at everything in government that should be respected!" With sardonic humor, Scherr comments, "Who would not have heeded the firm decision of this poor locksmith-king? Never, said he, would the comedy be performed; so what happened on April 27, 1784? *The Marriage of Figaro* was performed at the Théâtre Français to jubilant acclaim!"

Beaumarchais, leaving no stone unturned, had started a real conspiracy among the ministers, courtiers, prelates, members of parliament, and even the Queen until his play was given. The "horrid play" attracted such masses of spectators that three people suffocated in the crowds milling in front of the theater. Beaumarchais ordered that the fiftieth performance should be a benefit for the poor of Paris; the creator of *Figaro,* Scherr observes, was always known as a tenderhearted man to whom the poor and lonely never appealed in vain. Kind and forgiving by nature, he extended his generosity even to his enemies. Of course, he was attacked bitterly, especially by other writers; in answer to one of the literary critics who plagued him, he wrote loftily, "Do you really think that after conquering lions and tigers to have my comedy performed, I would stoop to punish a mere insect?"

Beaumarchais's glory ended, ironically enough, with

the start of the revolution his plays had helped to kindle. He had to flee Paris and remained in exile until 1796. Wryly he remarked, on his return, "Here I am, a good old man, great, gray, obese and fat." Though he rejoiced in the favor of Napoleon, the Corsican valued, not the author who had had the courage to pen *Figaro,* but the one who wrote the more emotional but less controversial or witty *La Mère Coupable.* Years later in exile on St. Helena, Napoleon described *Figaro* as "the revolution already in action" and condemned it at the same time. Author Scherr asks, "Could the great despot, even after his downfall, not stand the thought of opposition?"

"Beaumarchais died a lonely death. Peace and serenity were on his face, a peace he had never enjoyed in life. . . . The Great Reaper had led him to rest, he who comes to all at the end, when the aged children become tired, when their busy hands drop and their feverish brains stop working. . . ." Thus Scherr, in a poetic vein, brings to a close his life of Beaumarchais, the relentless fighter for whom Cleon's words in *Le Méchant* may serve as a motto: "Fools are here below for our sheer amusement." Or perhaps we should remember Susanna's speech: "Joy I love, because it is so foolish!"

Revolutionary Figaro

BY JANE W. STEDMAN

"Way for the Factotum of the City," cries Figaro. He might well have added, "And way for the French Revolution," for he was, in the dramas of Beaumarchais, to say nothing of his operatic descendants, a harbinger of the New Age.

Figaro, as we know, has his origin in the comedies of Pierre Augustin Caron de Beaumarchais, a watchmaker's son who underwent adventures as fabulous as those of his literary counterpart, and whose life and work contributed to the overthrow of that aristocracy which he presented with such charm and such cynicism. That Beaumarchais considered Figaro (whom Henri Lion called "the stage hero of the Revolution") to be a projection of himself is suggested by the name he gave to his other self: Figaro—an old pronunciation, slightly slurred, of *fils Caron,* or Caron's son.* Moreover, the barber's interest in rising in life, his

* This explanation originates with Lintilhac.

gay impudence, his ingenuity, particularly his deft hand at intrigue, all suggest his creator's personality. Beaumarchais, born Pierre Caron, first came to the attention of the French court through a dispute over his invention of a clever mechanism, later used in a tiny ring-watch for Madame Pompadour, a bauble which became the "rage" of the court. It was not long before the young man acquired a wife (who died soon) and a new name—de Beaumarchais —from her estate. Soon he was instructing the daughters of Louis XV in playing the pedal harp, an occupation which must have an echo in the lesson scene of *The Barber of Seville,* to say nothing of the hints his new life was providing for the Count and Countess of *The Marriage of Figaro.*

Beaumarchais, now more than affluent, added new experiences to his growing fund for plays when in 1764 he went to Spain to straighten out a love affair of his sister's, an episode full of the intrigue beloved by both author and character. As well as absorbing local color for his future comedy, Beaumarchais was also acting in Spain as a secret agent, a career which stretched over a period of years and countries, interspersed with plays—first, domestic problem dramas and then his Figaro series, beginning with the *Barber of Seville.*

The production of this comedy took place under a confusion of difficulties ranging from an actor's prejudiced pride to official disfavor and repression. First of these was the refusal of the Comédiens Italiens to take the Barber (then in comic opera form) because Clairval, the stage idol of the day, had himself been a barber and refused to appear on stage in that character. More important was the official disapproval Beaumarchais was undergoing in a suit against Goëzmann, a judge who had taken his bribes without honor or satisfaction, and who had denounced the dramatist before Parliament. Now Beaumarchais felt the calumny celebrated by Don Basilio. His retaliation took the form of coruscating pamphlets in which Goëzmann and the courts of law were scored off in wit so brilliant that six thousand copies were sold in three days. The upshot of the affair was a return to "secret missions" for Beaumarchais and a canceled production for the *Barber* on suspicion that it satirized judges. Finally on February 23, 1775, the *Barber,* now a comedy only, was presented at the Comédie Française with an opening night which disappointed both audience and author. A revision of the play, however, was made for the second performance which proved its salvation and success.

But if *The Barber of Seville* was Beaumarchais and Figaro in merry and ultimately optimistic mood, *The Marriage of Figaro* (or *La Folle Journée,* to give it its original title), performed in 1784, found both of them far more bitter, with iron beneath their golden jests and the far-off rumble of tumbrils under their dancing measures. *The Marriage of Figaro* was, beneath its madcap plot, so iconoclastic a play that even the proverbially dull Louis XVI personally prohibited its presentation.

In the *Marriage,* Beaumarchais contended not merely

that a lackey imitated his master (such imitation had been a stage convention for a century), but that "in knowledge and character" the servant was often superior to the master. As a practical example the dramatist had himself risen from obscurity through his own wit and resourcefulness, owing nothing to lineage. Figaro's bitter soliloquy in Act V sums up Beaumarchais's attitude toward unmeritorious nobility in the person of Almaviva. "Because you are a great lord, you think yourself a great genius!" cries Figaro. "Nobility, fortune, rank, offices. . . . What have you done for so many blessings? You have given yourself the trouble of being born, that's all; aside from that, you're ordinary enough! While I! lost in the obscure crowd, have had to employ more knowledge and more wit merely to exist. . . ." Truly this is a revolutionary speech implying as it does the instrinsic worthlessness of aristocracy.

More folly, however, than the superficiality of rank was attacked by the dramatist. Chamfort, who read the play in manuscript, thought it presented every foible of the age, the vital issues of the day, law, politics, metaphysics, in laughing scenes with serious undercurrents. Ironically enough *The Marriage of Figaro* at last reached the stage because of court sponsorship. When told of the King's opposition Beaumarchais is said to have declared, "If there is no other obstacle, my play will be produced." Whereupon he sent men and boys to the streets to whistle a tune incorporated in the comedy. This opposition to Louis aroused the whimsical fancy of the court, whose motto soon became: "There can be no salvation without *The Marriage of Figaro.*" * With unconscious irony they patronized their destruction. Even international relations entered the conflict, Grand Duke Paul, son of Catherine the Great, in France with his wife, wanted to hear the new *Figaro.*

At last on April 27, 1784, hundreds of people of all classes packed the street in a near-riot for tickets to the first public performance of the *Marriage.* Napoleon, looking back much later, declared that its success was "the Revolution approaching." † And it came on rapidly even though another explosion of royal wrath sent Beaumarchais to prison for six days, and even though Marie Antoinette afterward enacted Rosine in a Trianon performance of the *Barber* with the Count d'Artois as Figaro. This private production, at which the dramatist was present, was the operatic version of the play by Paisiello, whose music died away before the familiar Rossini setting of 1816. The amateur operatic evening took place two days after the arrest of Cardinal de Rohan in the diamond necklace scandal.

Now the Revolution was arising, and in its midst Beaumarchais, who had contributed to its spirit and strength, was afraid. Although born of the people, his fortune had been cast in courts, and as aristocracy declined so did the satirist of aristocracy. Yet in the whirlwind of 1792 he

* Quoted by P. Frischauer, translated by M. Goldsmith.
† *Ibid.*

brought out his last play on the Figaro theme and characters, *La Mère Coupable*. In this his purpose was to evoke tears, not laughter, and it proved a poor third to its sparkling forerunners, in spite of achieving 114 performances in approximately sixty years.

Before the production of *La Mère Coupable*, however, Beaumarchais had been employed by the revolutionary government to secure guns from Holland (he had supplied arms during the American Revolution nearly twenty years before), had failed, and had been denounced before the National Assembly. The friendship of the Procurator's mistress helped to free Beaumarchais, and his imprisoned wife, sister, and daughter were saved only by the ending of the Terror. The aging dramatist took cold refuge in a debtor's prison in England, from whence he wrote another inflammatory pamphlet. He returned to France for the last time in 1796 when the Directory had replaced the Convention. Then he found himself once more acclaimed, permitted to engage in public life, and finally to die quietly, as secure in his position as Figaro who, his Revolutionary purpose satisfied, has never ceased to fulfill his comic destiny.

The Battle of *Figaro*

BY ANN M. LINGG

When Mozart quit the service of the Salzburg Archbishop
to become a freelance musician in Vienna, he was confident
that his talents would provide him with a decent living
and protect him against humiliation. He could hardly have
foreseen that far greater annoyances than those suffered
in Salzburg would begin to harass him as soon as he entered into competition with the Italians on the Emperor's
musical staff.

Key figure among the anti-Mozart forces was Court Conductor Antonio Salieri, a protégé of the venerable Gluck.
Suave, career-minded, and clever, and only six years Mozart's senior, the Italian held the most coveted musical
position in Vienna, if not in Europe, and he was well on
his guard against the insignificant-looking young pianist
from the provinces, whose tremendous genius impressed
and frightened him. Salieri was no real villain, as many
Mozart biographers would have it; and he certainly did

not poison Mozart, as legend formerly related. But he was a shrewd schemer who used all the prerogatives of his office to put Mozart in his place. He not only tried to keep him away from the opera, by fair means or foul; he even jeopardized Mozart's appointment as piano teacher to Archduke Francis' fiancée, thus depriving his rival of a badly needed income, with no material advantage to himself.

One real clash might have cleared the air; but there was no open conflict between Mozart and Salieri. They were studiedly polite in personal intercourse, but Mozart was at a permanent disadvantage. He lacked the official title, flair for intrigue, and impressive appearance of the Italian maestro. Later, as he grew even poorer and sicker, his distrust of Salieri became an obsession and embittered his life to his last hour. He never even suspected that Salieri was afraid of *him*.

Although prepared to make his living as a pianist and instrumental composer, Mozart wanted nothing so much as to write for the stage. When he arrived in Vienna, Joseph II was just sponsoring opera in Germany, and in 1782 Mozart wrote *The Abduction from the Seraglio* for the Court Theater. Soon thereafter, however, the *Singspiel* company was dissolved, and Salieri persuaded the Emperor to have the theater reorganized along Italian lines.

Impresario Count Orsini-Rosenberg sent scouts all over Italy and hired the best singers they could find. With this superb new company, Italian opera in Vienna reached another peak of popularity. Mozart went hunting for a suitable libretto, but could not find one he liked. And while Italian composers, poets, and singers flocked to Vienna, the composer of *Idomeneo* remained an outsider at the opera house.

It was fortunate for Mozart, and for us who bask in the beauties of *Figaro, Don Giovanni, Così Fan Tutte,* that the Italians in Vienna did not get along with each other. Had there been no discord in the Italian camp, Salieri might have forever monopolized his protégé, Lorenzo da Ponte, for whom he had obtained the post of court poet after Metastasio's death. But it so happened that their *Il Ricco d'un giorno* (Rich for a day) was a dismal flop, while only a few short months before, Paisiello's *Il Re Teodoro* had been signally successful. And *Il Re*'s librettist was the brilliant and notorious Abbate Casti, who had settled in Vienna determined to supplant Da Ponte, whom he considered an upstart and a greenhorn at libretto writing— both of which happened to be true.

Casti, backed by his old friend Rosenberg, smirked at the failure of *Il Ricco*. His friends poured venom on Da Ponte, and the singers stood up as one man against the librettist. Salieri swore that he would cut off his hand rather than set another line of Da Ponte's verse. And the court poet, who had become a librettist without a composer, suddenly remembered that Mozart, the favorite of the concert platform, was still a composer without a librettist.

In retrospect it does not seem surprising that this oddly

assorted pair finally joined in a partnership that produced
the finest gems in the treasure of opera. But when their
teamwork started, the machinations of the hostile clique
were so powerful that the Emperor in person had to interfere three times to rescue *Figaro* from being strangled at
birth.

The idea for *Figaro* originated with Mozart, who had become enamored of Beaumarchais's rambling play. Da Ponte
cleverly managed to omit all offensive passages, and after
hearing some of the music, Joseph II ordered the performance. His Italian musicians, however, tried every trick
in the book to circumvent the command.

First began a fight for priority. Both Salieri and one
Vincenzo Righini had operas ready, and Rosenberg insisted that *Figaro* would have to wait. Righini incited
clandestine intrigues; three leading singers campaigned for
Salieri; Mozart was backed by his Irish tenor friend,
Michael O'Kelly, whose *Reminiscences* give a vivid account of the battle of *Figaro*. "[The rivalry] raised much
discord and parties were formed," he relates. "Every one in
the opera company took part in . . . the mighty contest
[which] was put an end to by His Majesty issuing a man-
date for *Figaro* to be instantly put into rehearsal."

Next, a Salieri partisan informed Rosenberg that Da
Ponte had introduced a ballet into the third act, even
though an imperial decree banned dancers from the Court
Theater. Rosenberg was triumphant. He summoned Da
Ponte and, on the poet's refusal to eliminate the scene,
threw the sheets containing it in the fire.

But the brief scene in *Figaro* is no ballet in the ordinary sense; it is a dramatic requisite, providing the background for a mute play between Susanna and the Count, which establishes the plot of the final act. Da Ponte succeeded in having the Emperor with his retinue attend the dress rehearsal. When it came to the crucial scene, the orchestra stopped playing. There was no ballet, but there was no music either. "All one could notice was Susanna and the Count gesticulating. . . . It looked like a puppet show," Da Ponte recorded in his *Memoirs*. The thing made no sense at all.

"What do you think this means?" Joseph asked Casti who sat behind him.

"Your Majesty ought to ask the poet," Casti sneered.

Da Ponte, quickly summoned, handed the Emperor the manuscript, in which the scene had been restored. The Emperor wondered why the dances were not performed. Da Ponte remained ominously silent. "There are no dancers in this theater, since Your Majesty does not want them," stammered an uneasy Rosenberg.

"Aren't there dancers in other theaters?" Joseph asked.

The ballet was reinstated, but the Salieri clique, angrier than ever, did not give up. At the premiere, some of the singers obliged by deliberately ruining the first act. They sang off pitch, omitted lines, missed cues. But Joseph II had a fine ear, for both music and rebellion. His displeasure was communicated to Rosenberg, together with a warning that the future of the Italian company would depend on a satisfactory performance of *Figaro*.

Mozart had won. The public demanded so many encores that the performance lasted nearly twice as long as had been expected. "Never has anything been more complete than the triumph of Mozart and his *Figaro*," exulted O' Kelly.

It was a Pyrrhic victory, however. After the premiere, *da capos* were prohibited, allegedly in order not to overstrain the singers; and after nine performances the work was shelved. And Emperor Joseph, harassed by far weightier problems than operas and their composers, no longer interfered. Mozart was no better off than before.

And yet, *Figaro* marks the turning point in his opera career. Its sensational success in Prague led to *Don Giovanni*, its revival in Vienna, in 1789, to *Così*. And Salieri, despite the kindness he showed as an older man to the young Beethoven, Schubert, and Liszt, might have been relegated to the long list of wholesale composers of pleasant music, had he not gone down in history as the evil spirit in Mozart's brief and troubled life.

Da Ponte and the Bussanis

BY LLOYD HARRIS

When the librettist of a new opera describes its leading soprano as "an Italian *diva* who, though a ridiculous person of little merit, had by dint of facial contortions, clown's tricks and perhaps by means more theatrical still, built up a great following among cooks, barbers, lackeys, butlers and hostlers, and in consequence was thought a gem"— and that opera has had a dazzling success, it is just as well to look into the matter!

Lorenzo da Ponte did not write these lines about Dorotea Bussani in connection with her interpretation of Cherubino at the premiere of *Le Nozze di Figaro*. They were provoked, rather, by irritation at her husband, Francesco Bussani, a bass singer, comedian, and backstage intriguer. In the various forms of political maneuver that flourish in an opera house, the sides can shift at any moment. The Bussanis, however, invariably found themselves arrayed counter to Da Ponte—not a very comfortable place, perhaps, since it was constantly menaced by the poet's power of invective and close connection with the Emperor Joseph II.

Still, Da Ponte might not have bothered with Dorotea and Francesco Bussani, as unimportant members of the opera company and more irritating than influential in the various plots and cabals of the imperial theater at Vienna, had not Dorotea—with the very bag of tricks which Da Ponte found so odious—somehow managed to establish a certain rivalry with Adriana Gabrielli-Del Bene. This great singer, who created the demanding role of Fiordiligi, was not only a popular favorite but the mistress of Da Ponte. Such a rivalry, to his mind, savored of *lèse majesté*.

Thus in Da Ponte's *Memoirs*, Francesco Bussani's morals and Dorotea's art are torn to shreds. Michael Kelly, writing of the same epoch, had little to say about these people: he includes them in the enthusiastic praise he extended to all who participated in *Le Nozze di Figaro*, mentions Dorotea's singing in Paisiello's *Il Re Teodoro* and implies that Francesco was among the large bloc of singers who favored shelving *Figaro* in favor of Salieri's *La Grotta di Trofonio* or an unspecified opera by Vincenzo Righini.

The troupe assembled for the theater at Vienna was undoubtedly a powerful one. Antonio Salieri was chief conductor, Da Ponte official librettist, and the singers included Nancy Storace, Aloysia Lange, Laura Caterina Cavalieri (German, despite her name), Adriana Gabrielli-Del Bene, Michael Kelly, Stefano Mandini, and Benucci. Judging by the music Mozart wrote for some of these singers in *Le Nozze di Figaro* and *Così Fan Tutte*, they must have been lavishly endowed vocalists. Mozart understood the voice well and always got along with singers; there is every reason to believe that he tailored his output to the qualifications of the individual artists. Such being the case, one can draw a fairly clear picture of the Bussanis' talents.

Dorotea was evidently a clever comedienne with a soprano voice of short range. Cherubino, as we know, is nowadays sung as often by a mezzo-soprano as by a soprano, the important thing being the plausibility of the characterization and the ability to project the two arias with grace and charm. Despina in *Così* is invariably sung by a light soprano; the brittle cynicisms of that character would probably evaporate if uttered by a mellow voice. Her two arias are not extended very far into the high part of the voice, but the general tessitura would be very difficult for any but a light soprano.

Francesco's opportunities were less spectacular. Doctor Bartolo is a stock *buffo* role, running far behind Figaro and Count Almaviva. Vocally the role does not ask for a great deal, and it deteriorates dramatically as the opera progresses. Doubling as Antonio probably gave Francesco something of a challenge in the matter of characterization, yet his contribution to *Le Nozze di Figaro* was not of the sort to make or break the show. Great artists can lift these roles out of the routine category by force of personality, exceptional voice, or inspired acting, but there is no evidence that Francesco achieved any such *tour de force*.

It is interesting to remark that Da Ponte never dignified Francesco Bussani with an artistic appraisal. He had been a member of the anti-Da Ponte clique from the very start, agitating in favor of Giambattista Casti as court poet, making trouble for Mozart and Da Ponte even up to the moment of the dress rehearsal of *Le Nozze* (Da Ponte says Mozart wanted to give Bussani a beating at that time) and thereafter insinuating himself into every situation inimical to the librettist up to the very moment Da Ponte was forced to leave Vienna. But while Da Ponte wrote, "There was a certain Bussani, who had a post as inspector of costumes and stage properties, and was jack-at-all-trades save at that of an honest man," he never honored him with comment, even adverse, on his stage appearances. Yet Bussani, in addition to Bartolo, Antonio, and Don Alfonso—which he created—also sang the first performances of the Commendatore and Masetto when *Don Giovanni* was given in Vienna.

This abstinence from comment on Da Ponte's part puts Bussani in the same class with Benucci and Mandini, the greatest *bassi buffi* of the period. Da Ponte, however, enjoys making an oblique allusion to Dorotea's partiality for the Spanish composer Martin y Solar (Martini).

The last reference Da Ponte makes to the couple who so persistently irritated him is a quotation from the Emperor Leopold II. Following the death of Joseph II, Da Ponte lost his position at court and was ordered to leave Vienna.

Accordingly he sought out the new emperor at Trieste and tried to smooth the way for a return. In the course of the interview the emperor (strangely paraphrasing Da Ponte's words of an earlier date) is quoted as saying, "Then there's Bussani! Bussani is a regular rascal. But he will learn to know me. I have found a certain Madame Gaspari in Venice. She will chase the grasshoppers out of the head of that insolent rope-jumper he has for a wife, even though her vulgar jokes, her clown's tricks, her raucous screams off-key have won her quite a claque among the barbers, cooks and messenger boys of my sweet Vienna. I have warned Gaspari not to give any leading role to that woman. If that doesn't work we'll find other ways. . . ."

Such words suggest Da Ponte himself more than Leopold. The Bussanis were not the greatest of the poet's enemies nor the last. After his failure to regain his post in Vienna, they were among the group who victoriously remained. Nor were they, so far as we know, among those enemies whose fate comforted Da Ponte. One was hanged, one was struck by lightning, one went to prison, one died a beggar. Not so the Bussanis. Their punishment—or reward—lay in having been immortalized in some of Da Ponte's choice passages of vituperation.

Michael Kelly

BY PAUL NETTL

The eighteenth century was a period of scribbling. Everybody wrote. Goethe, the great poet, encouraged his contemporaries to write their autobiographies. Schiller spoke of the "ink blotting *saeculum.*" Intellectual men and women left no scrap of paper uninscribed to record their experiences, no matter how banal.

The greatest writers of memoirs of the period were Goethe, Goldoni, Casanova, Da Ponte, and Madame de Staël. But lesser spirits who described their experiences and encounters with men and women of the theatrical and musical world are also interesting for their history of culture and music. Among these "extras" on the historical stage was the Irish singer Michael Kelly, whose reminiscences, which appeared in London in 1826, are among the most important sources for the history of music in the late eighteenth century. His notations are particularly valuable for us because in Vienna, as imperial singer, he came in intimate contact with Mozart and his circle.

Born in Dublin at Christmastide 1762, the son of the
wine merchant and dancing master Thomas Kelly, he
showed as a boy a decided talent for music. His father,
anxious for adequate instruction for his son, had him take
piano lessons with Morland (1770–72) and Michael Arne
(1777–78), and entrusted the lovely voice of the youth to
singing masters like Passerini, Peretti, and St. Giorgio.

Kelly also studied with Matteo Rauzzini (1754–81),
brother of a famous singer, who had settled in Dublin
and gave singing lessons. It was he who prevailed upon
Kelly's parents to send the boy to Italy.

Before the boy started his great journey, he had the opportunity of appearing on the Dublin stage. He sang the
Count in Piccinni's opera *La Buona Figliuola,* the hero
in Michael Arne's opera *Cymon,* and other roles. He met
a group of important musicians, including the oboist
Johann Christian Fischer (1733–1800).

Fischer, who was much admired by his contemporaries
because of the particularly good tone he got from his instrument, was also well acquainted with Mozart, who
raked him over the coals but nevertheless composed his
Twelve Variations for him. This minuet, as Kelly expresses it, became "all the rage." Fischer was on friendly
terms with the painter Gainsborough, whose charming
daughter he married. The painter also made a portrait of
the oboist; the beautiful picture still hangs in Bucking-
ham Palace. He must have been a witty man, for Kelly relates the following neat little incident about him, an an-

ecdote that was later applied to other artists: Being
pressed by a nobleman to sup with him after the opera, he
declined the invitation, saying that he was usually very
much fatigued and made it a rule never to go out after
the evening's performance. The noble lord would, however, take no denial, and assured Fischer that he did not
ask him professionally but merely for the gratification of
his society and conversation. Thus urged and encouraged,
he went; he had not, however, been many minutes in the
house of the insistent nobleman before his lordship ap-
proached him and said, "I hope, Mr. Fischer, you have
brought your oboe in your pocket?"

"No, my Lord," said Fischer, "my oboe never sups." He
turned on his heel and instantly left the house, and no
persuasion could ever induce him to return to it.

Kelly went to Naples, the voyage taking place during the
American war. "The ship I was on board of, being a
Swede, was under a neutral flag; yet in the Bay of Biscay
we were hailed by an American privateer. Our captain lay
to, while a set of the greatest ragamuffins my eyes ever
beheld boarded us. They swore the vessel was under false
colors and proceeded to overhaul the captain's papers, and
seize everything they could lay hands on. A sturdy ruffian
began to break open my pianoforte case with a hatchet
which, when I saw, I manfully began to weep and cry out:
'Oh! my dear pianoforte.' The cabin boy, who was about
my own age, called out, 'For God's sake, don't cry, Master
Kelly.'

"The chief mate of the privateer, who was quietly perusing some of our Captain's papers, on hearing these words, turned round and looking steadfastly at me, said: 'Is your name Kelly?'

"I answered, 'Yes.'

" 'Do you know anything of a Mr. Thomas Kelly, of Mary Str., Dublin?' he said.

" 'He is my father,' was my reply.

"The young man immediately started up, ran to me, clasped me in his arms, and with tears in his eyes, said, 'Don't you remember me? I am Jack Cunningham, who, when you were a little boy, nursed you and played with you.' ". . .

The climax of Kelly's career was his stay in Vienna, his appointment to the opera of the Emperor Joseph II, and his friendship with Mozart. After all kinds of adventures in Florence, Venice, and Leghorn and a somewhat unsuccessful appointment in Graz, Kelly came to Vienna in 1783 after he had been recommended by his patron, Count Orsini-Rosenberg. The first thing he did was visit the great Italian opera composer Antonio Salieri (1750–1825), at that time second director of the opera. Salieri became Kelly's superior. He informed Kelly that his own opera, *La Scuola dei Gelosi,* was to be the first production, in which Michael would make his debut.

Of course, Kelly was primarily interested in the merry, colorful social life of the Austrian capital. The Prater, which he compares with Hyde Park, the famous *Back-*

hendeln (fried chickens), the renowned Viennese carnival with its masquerades and balls in which the waltz, at that time completely unknown in England, played a great part, the theatrical events—all this is described in detail in Kelly's memoirs.

In Naples, where Kelly settled, he studied under the singing master Finarolo, at that time director of the conservatory La Madonna di Loreto. His principal teacher, however, was the famous castrato and contralto Giuseppe Aprile (1738–1814), with whom Cimarosa had also studied. It is to Aprile that Kelly owed his career as a singer. Soon he performed in various opera houses. He traveled to Sicily, stopped in Rome, and kept his eyes open for what he could see of the country and the people. Of course, his views were directed principally to the opera, and I should not like to omit his merry description of the manner in which the Romans criticized singers. "The numerous abbés were the severest of the critics; they would sit in the front of the pit, each bearing in one hand a lighted wax taper and in the other the score of the opera, and should an unfortunate singer make a mistake, the critical clerics would call out *'Brava bestia'* ('Bravo, you beast')! The composer of the opera used to preside at the pianoforte during the first three performances of his work, and a bad time he often had of it. Should any passage of his opera strike the audience as similar to the melody of another composer, the cry would arise: *'Bravo, il ladro!'* ('Bravo, you thief') or *'Bravo, Paisiello!'* *'Bravo Sacchini,'* if they considered the passage stolen from these masters."

These words remind us of the famous banquet scene from Mozart's *Don Giovanni*, when the orchestra plays melodies from different operas in vogue at that time. *"Bravo Cosa rara!" "Evvivano i 'Litiganti'!"* calls Leporello, the Don's comical servant.

In the scintillating abundance of his memories, music takes the first place. Kelly paid a visit to Haydn, living at that time in Eisenstadt with Prince Esterházy. Three days he stayed with the composer, and Kelly assures us that it was a pleasure of the first rank to go riding with Haydn in the elegant coach of the Prince, to see the vicinity of Eisenstadt. One day Kelly went to a concert in which the famous Kozebuch played the piano. "What was to me," so he writes, "one of the greatest gratifications of my musical life, I was then introduced to that prodigy of genius—Mozart. He favored the company by performing fantasias and capriccios on the pianoforte. His feeling, the rapidity of his fingers, the great execution and strength of his left hand particularly, and the apparent inspiration of his modulations astounded me. After this splendid performance, we sat down to supper and I had the pleasure to be placed at a table between him and his wife, Madame Constance Weber, a German lady of whom he was passionately fond, and by whom he had three children."

As one of Mozart's most striking characteristics Kelly mentions his fondness for the dance. Mme. Mozart, according to Kelly, once insisted that "his taste lay in that art rather than in music"—certainly a peculiar remark of the good Constance. "He was," so Kelly continued, "a remarkably small man, very thin and pale with a profusion of fine hair, of which he was rather vain. He gave me a cordial invitation to his home, of which I availed myself, and passed a great part of my time there. He always received me with kindness and hospitality. He was remarkably fond of punch, of which beverage I have seen him take copious draughts. He was also fond of billiards, and had an excellent billiard table in his house. Many and many a game have I played with him, but always came off second best. He gave Sunday concerts, at which I was never missing. He was kind-hearted and always ready to oblige, but so very particular, when he played, that if the slightest noise were made, he instantly left off."

Kelly, flattered by Mozart's recognition, relates that he composed a couple of arias and showed them to the master. "He kindly approved them, so much indeed, that I determined to devote myself to composition." Kelly wished to train himself better in counterpoint and asked Mozart for advice as to a teacher. Mozart was of the opinion he should continue as a writer of melodies, for melody was Kelly's real field of talent. Besides, Mozart said, his career as an opera singer really occupied all his endeavors. A writer of melody, observed Mozart, was to be compared with a race horse, a contrapuntist with a dependable coach horse.

It is interesting that Kelly had an important role in the history of Mozart's operas. In the premiere of *The Marriage of Figaro,* May 1, 1786, he sang the role of Basilio in the Burgtheater. Mozart esteemed the versatile tenor highly for both serious and comical roles. He was an excellent actor, and relates that this talent once filled the famous librettist Casti, as well as Paisiello, with such enthusiasm that they gave him the difficult part of Gafforino in *Re Teodoro,* in which he enjoyed great success.

In planning the various roles of *Figaro,* Mozart doubtless took into consideration the individuality of his performers. Kelly—or O'Kelly, as he called himself in Vienna, and as his name appears in the autograph of Mozart in the libretto—reports: "In the second act sextet, I had a very conspicuous part, as the stuttering judge, Basilio. All through the piece I was to stutter, but in the sextet, Mozart requested I would not, for if I did I should spoil his music. I told him, that although it might appear very presumptuous of a lad like me to differ from him on this point, I did, and was sure that the way in which I intended to introduce the stuttering would not interfere with the other parts, but produce an effect. Besides it certainly was not in nature that I should stutter all through the part and when I came to the sextet speak plain; and after that piece of music was over, return to stuttering, and I added, apologizing at the same time for my apparent want of deference and respect in placing my opinion in opposition to that of the great Mozart, that unless I was allowed to perform the part as I wished, I would not perform it at all. Mozart at last consented that I should have my own way, but doubted the success of the experiment. Crowded

houses proved that nothing on the stage ever produced a
more powerful effect; the audience were convulsed with
laughter, in which Mozart himself joined. The Emperor
repeatedly cried out: Bravo! and the piece was loudly applauded and encored. When the opera was over, Mozart
came on the stage to me, and shaking my both hands, said:
'Bravo, young man, I feel obliged to you; and acknowledge
you have been in the right, and myself in the wrong'." . . .

Kelly was not the only singer from the British Isles appearing in *Figaro,* for the feminine leading part of the
opera, the charming Susanna, was in the hands of the Eng-
lishwoman Nancy Storace (1766–1817). Nancy's father had
come to Italy from Ireland, where the family had become
completely Anglicized. Kelly gives an amusing report of
how Stephen Storace and his sister, the singer, met him on
a voyage to Leghorn. Michael, who as a blond and rather
boyish-looking young man might have been taken for a
disguised girl, heard how one of the passengers, a girl, said
in English to her companion, "Look at that girl dressed
in boys' clothes." To her astonishment Kelly called out, in
the same language, "You are mistaken, Miss. I am a very
proper he animal, and quite at your service."

All three laughed immoderately and from that moment
was formed a firm friendship which was to have important
developments in the musical world of the coming years.
Stephen Storace became a respected composer in Vienna
at the same time as Kelly, and likewise a pupil of Mozart's.
He wrote a number of chamber music works of excellent
construction.

In February 1787, Kelly departed from Vienna. The Emperor granted him a year's vacation with pay, but he never came back. With Kelly traveled his English friends, Thomas Attwood (likewise a pupil of Mozart's) and the brother and sister Storace. Stephen Storace the evening before had had an encounter with an officer because the latter, at a ball, while he was wearing a saber and spears, had danced with Nancy—something which the English musician, who had drunk too freely of Buda wine, thought sufficient reason for insulting the officer. Storace had to spend a night in jail but was released through Kelly's intervention with the Emperor, so that the group might depart.

Taking leave from Mozart must have been painful. When the travelers passed Salzburg they stopped at father Leopold Mozart's place on the Hannibalplatz to give him greetings from his son.

Mozart's English friends had tried with might and main to induce the master to come to England. Mozart had almost made up his mind to do so, since Vienna was ungrateful and little appreciative of his music. The somewhat frivolous Mme. Mozart even wanted to send her children off to her father-in-law in Salzburg to be cared for, but Leopold refused energetically. His lack of cooperation and the negotiations starting with the Prague opera producer Guardasoni, who invited Mozart to come to the Bohemian capital, were the reasons for the composer making up his mind to stay in Vienna.

And Kelly? His Viennese days were the climax of his

career. What later followed was only an echo of that glorious time. He became first tenor in the Drury Lane Theater in London. He sang in the concerts of the Society of Ancient Music in the Handel performances at Westminster Abbey. He had not, however, forgotten that Mozart had thought highly of his canzonettas. He wrote songs and music for plays. When he had lost his voice he became theater director and opened a music store; but since his business sense was not notable, he soon went bankrupt. Because selling wines was traditional in his family, and he had acquired a knowledge of good wine in Italy and Austria, he opened up a wine establishment in 1811. This fact and the prevalent opinion in London that Kelly leaned too much on other composers as models, and diluted his wine a bit, is supposed to have been the cause for Sheridan's famous statement that the sign over Kelly's business establishment should have read

Michael Kelly
COMPOSER OF WINES
AND
IMPORTER OF MUSIC

Figaro Dressed for Paris

BY CHRISTOPHER RAEBURN

A question which has puzzled scholars and producers is the exact nature of the first production of Mozart's *Le Nozze di Figaro,* particularly in relation to its costumes and scenery.

The information is almost as meager as that for *Così Fan Tutte.* Both Da Ponte and Michael Kelly, the original Don Basilio and Don Curzio, have left their versions of the preparations and intrigues leading up to the opening performance, but these well-known accounts throw little light on the question of the setting. There are no pictorial records of the original production nor of any actual scene from Mozart's *Figaro* during the whole of the eighteenth century, except for the possibility of one suspect drawing, sometimes reproduced as "Garden Scene from *Le Nozze di Figaro.*" There is no evidence to believe that this drawing had anything to do with the Vienna performance, and its date is uncertain.

So we are left to draw on what evidence is available,

though any hypothesis arising out of it should not be taken as actual fact. The opera was well into rehearsal by April, 1786, and received its first performance on the first of May. It was performed by the Italian Opera Company of the National Theater in Vienna. Though the personnel of the German Opera Company and the Theater (legitimate) Company were different, they all came under the same management, composed of certain of the actors themselves and a handful of officials. There was certainly no stage director as we know the position today, and no official theater architect-designer like Quaglio in Munich. It seems that costumes and scenery were not given special importance. Theater criticisms, and diarists noted for their descriptions of sumptuously presented productions such as took place under Schikaneder's management, remain silent over the décor of the National Theater.

Though the Beaumarchais *Le Mariage de Figaro* had not yet been performed in Vienna, his play *Le Barbier de Séville* and Paisiello's opera *Il Barbiere di Siviglia* were in the repertory of the National Theater. And Beaumarchais is possibly more specific in his costume instructions than any other playwright of his time. In the 1776 German translation of the Beaumarchais *Barbier,* there is the following introductory note: "The Actors must be dressed in old Spanish costume."

The only pointer we have about the first performance of Mozart's *Figaro* is the introduction to the libretto. Here Da Ponte excuses the length of the piece, explains his extensive adaptation of the Beaumarchais, which omits the whole of Act III (the Trial Scene), and finally states "our special purpose, which was to offer a new type of show, as it were, to a public of such refined taste and such assured understanding." If this preface referred to a new visual presentation of the piece, it is likely that it would have been recorded either then or in connection with later performances. We know of no such record. Although Da Ponte stresses that he is presenting something *new,* the novelty was probably in the length of the piece, and it must be remembered that the preface was in itself a tactful gesture to the court to disassociate the opera from the so-called revolutionary tendencies which made the play distasteful to the monarchy. Furthermore, Mozart's own realistic treatment of the characters was something quite new and transcended the conventional buffoonery or tragic aura surrounding operatic characters of the past.

There seems to be no direct indication of a departure from either the costumes or scenery of the Beaumarchais. We do know that German eighteenth-century productions of the opera retained the style of presentation they had used for the play of *Figaro,* and for want of further information it can be validly suggested that Vienna followed Beaumarchais in this respect. In view of this it is worthwhile reproducing Beaumarchais's own costume instructions from the first published edition of the play, as well as his character studies, which are of considerable relevance:

LE COMTE ALMAVIVA should be played aristocratically, but freely and with grace. The decadence of his heart should not affect his good breeding. In the manners of the time, the great treated any affair with the ladies as sport. This role is all the more difficult to play well, since the character is always sacrificed to the situation. But when played by a brilliant actor (M. Molé), he illumines all the other roles and assures the success of the piece.

His dress for the first and second acts is a riding habit with half-boots to the calf, in the style of old Spanish costume. From the third act to the end, a magnificent costume in the same style.

LA COMTESSE, torn between two conflicting emotions, should show only a restrained sensitivity or very moderate passion; above all nothing which degrades her kind and virtuous character in the eyes of the spectator. This role, one of the most difficult of the piece, has done infinite honor to the great talent of Mlle. Saint-Val the younger.

Her costume for the first, second and fourth acts is an informal plain gown, with no ornament on her head: she is at home and supposed to be indisposed. In the fifth act she has the same attire and high coiffure as Suzanne.

FIGARO. One cannot commend enough to the actor who would play this role well, to put his whole spirit into it, as M. Dazincourt has done. If he should see it another way than with the correct seasoning of gaiety and wit, above all if he should overplay it, he debases a role which, the leading comedian of our theatre had judged, does honor to the talent of every actor who should seize its innumerable nuances and can rise to its whole conception.

His costume as in *Le Barbier de Séville*. (Clothed as a Spanish valet. The head covered with a *rescille* or net; white hat,

a colored ribbon around the crown, a silk neckerchief tied
very loosely round the neck, satin waistcoat and breeches, with
buttons and buttonholes fringed with silver; a sash of silk,
garters knotted with tassels which hang on each leg; jacket
the same color as the waistcoat; white stockings and grey
shoes.)

SUZANNE, artful young person, witty and gay, but not of that
almost shameless gaiety of our soubrette corruptresses; her
pretty character is drawn in the preface, and it is this that
an actress who has never seen Mlle. Contat should study to
portray the part well.

Her costume for the first four acts is plain white *à bas-
quines,* very elegant, the skirt the same, with a bonnet lately
called by our tradesmen *à la Suzanne.* During the festivities
of the fourth act, the Count places on her head a long veiled
bonnet with high feathers and white ribbons. In the fifth act
she wears the informal dress of her mistress and is bare-
headed.

MARCELINE is a woman of spirit, born somewhat hot-headed,
but whose faults and experience have reformed her character. If the actress who plays her preens herself with pride,
which is justified by the very moral uplift following the recognition (of Figaro being her long-lost son) in the third
act, she will add greatly to the interest of the work.

Her costume is that of a Spanish duenna, of an unassum-
ing color, with a black bonnet on her head.

ANTONIO should only show a semi-drunkenness which is dis-
appearing by degrees, so that by the fifth act one can hardly
notice it.

His costume is that of a Spanish peasant, where the sleeves
hang behind; a hat and white shoes.

FANCHETTE (Barbarina) is a child of twelve, very naïve. Her simple dress is plain brown with bows and silver buttons, the skirt of a bright color, and a black bonnet with feathers. She should be dressed like the other peasants for the wedding.

CHÉRUBIN. This role can only be played as it has been, by a young and very pretty woman; we have not got in our theatre any very young men sufficiently trained to feel its finest points. Timid to the extreme in the presence of the Countess, otherwise a charming and mischievous child; a restless and indefinable desire is at the bottom of his character. He grows up to manhood, but without any plan or acquirements, and puts his whole being into every fresh incident; finally he is what every mother at the bottom of her heart would perhaps like her son to be, however much she had to suffer for it.

His rich costume for the first and second acts is that worn by a page of the Spanish court, white and embroidered with silver, with a light blue cloak on the shoulder and a hat laden with feathers. For the fourth act he has the bodice, skirt and bonnet of the young peasants who bring him in. For the fifth act, the uniform of an officer, with a cockade and sword.

BARTHOLO. The character and costume as in *Le Barbier de Séville;* he is here only a secondary role. (Short, buttoned black costume; large wig, ruff and ruffles turned up; a black sash; and when he wants to find his house, a long scarlet cloak.)

BAZILE. Character and costume as in *Le Barbier de Séville;* he is also here only a secondary role. (Flat black hat, short, cassock and long cloak without ruff or ruffles.)

BRID'OISON (a stuttering judge, but not altogether correspond-

ing in character to Don Curzio). His costume is the robe of a
Spanish judge, less full than those of our wigmakers, nearer
a cassock; a large wig, a Spanish neckband, and a long white
stick in his hand.

A PEASANT GIRL. Her costume like that of Fanchette.

PERSONAE MUTAE. Some dressed as judges (not applicable to
Mozart's *Figaro*), others in peasant costume and others in
livery.

These notes are of value to anyone interested in Mozart's
Figaro and indicate how Mozart and Da Ponte built up
their characters; Cherubino's first aria, "Non so più," is
directly inspired by Beaumarchais's remarks, which may
prove worthy of notice by anyone contemplating a production of the opera.

The Road to *Figaro*

BY BAIRD HASTINGS

We realize that Mozart was a miracle-maker in the theater, but how many of us are aware that the quality of rounded, disciplined completeness is found in his early operas for Milan and Munich? Let us consider his first twelve works for the theatter, placing them in a framework that will enable us to enjoy them for what they really are: youthful scores, full of the elements of inspiration later fused in the extraordinary masterworks of his final years.

Of Mozart's twenty-three works for the stage, fourteen are in Italian, seven in German; one is in Latin, and one is a ballet. Even in the Hapsburg Vienna court (and consequently in most of the lesser German courts as well) the official language of opera was Italian; so one is not surprised that Mozart's operas for Vienna and the German courts employ Italian texts, just as naturally as those created for Milanese carnivals or wedding celebrations. Only occasionally, when requested to write for a popular theater, was the composer given a German libretto. Then the form usually underwent changes: the gilded rococo style associated with court themes and Bibiena theaters was modified, and even the music took another tone.

Mozart's first stage works were the German opera-oratorio for which he wrote only the first act, *Die Schuldigkeit des ersten Gebotes* (The Observance of the First Commandment, K. 35), and the Ovid-based Latin comedy set in Sardinia, *Apollo et Hyacinthus,* written for insertion in a play performed at university exercises. Both these Handelian scores were focused on forgiveness—a favorite tenet of the philosophy of librettist Pietro Metastasio, which was, like liberty, important to Mozart all his life. Was the reiteration of the liberty theme part of the spirit of that era, or did it reflect Mozart's personal protest against the harshness of his Archbishop?

In a melody we may cite—No. 8 of *Die Schuldigkeit,* sung by the Christ Spirit—young Mozart appears already a master of lending urgency to his text, in this case "Action, it is folly to wait":

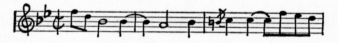

With *Bastien und Bastienne,* composed in 1768 after Jean Jacques Rousseau's *Devin du Village,* we come to a work already perfect on its own terms. Here is a story with an intriguing history, from such French musicians as Monsigny and Philidor through the Favarts (actors) to

Mozart. The plot—about two lovers brought together after a spat by the village soothsayer—may be simple, but it is characterized and developed well, and it speaks to any audience. One finds in the pastoral Bastienne a forerunner of the lovesick Pamina of *Zauberflöte;* one can compare the vain, misguided but basically sound Bastien with Belfiore in *La Finta Giardiniera;* the kindhearted Colas is Mozart's first master healer, of which type Sarastro represents the ultimate. *Bastien* was first produced in the Viennese garden of Dr. Anton Mesmer, an intimate of Casanova's and a lifelong friend of Mozart, who in *Così Fan Tutte* has Dr. Despina "mesmerize" back to life the Albanian lovers.

It was also in 1768 that Mozart composed his first Italian opera, *La Finta Semplice* (The Clever Flirt, or The Supposed Simpleton), a full-length work with twenty-five numbers. The Goldoni play (from which the libretto was adapted by Marco Coltellini, an Italian poet and librettist frequenting the Austrian court) offered seven characters whose nature induced amazing sophistication in Mozart's musical portraiture. While certain critics find this work an example of *opera buffa* akin to *commedia dell'arte,* the integration of text with music and of voice with orchestra indicates Mozart's original development as the work proceeds. In depicting each of the protagonists, too, he shows a range of insight that makes for suspense through three acts, right to the final curtain, when six of seven characters are "found married." In this opera we discover the first ser-

vant couple, types later so instrumental in the plots of
Finta Giardiniera, Entführung, Figaro, and *L'Oca del
Cairo.*

Mozart's philosophy (even if, at age twelve, he showed
it instinctively rather than encyclopedically) and his humility are what make his operas fresh and unhackneyed in
theme as well as musical structure. Almost never did he
repeat a formula that had proved successful for himself
or another composer; he conceived of each and every character as a changing, developing figure who must have personal individuality. As early as *La Finta Semplice* the
concerted finales make for a sophistication, a true round-
ing of the dramatic situation rare in eighteenth-century
opera. Consider, for example, Rosina's first aria, in which
the Baroness reflects on life and love; note with what
warmth Mozart paints her mood:

Because *La Finta Semplice* did not obtain a performance in the Hapsburg capital but was given a mediocre
staging in Salzburg, Mozart did not write another opera
for two years—though he often longed for the opportunity.
Mitridate, Re di Ponto, a three-act *dramma per musica,*
was composed for performance during the carnival season
in Milan in 1770. By traveling to several ducal courts in
Italy, Mozart father and son were able to prospect a commission with a libretto by the Turinese poet Vittorio

Amadeo Cigna-Santi, fashioned from Racine's tragedy. This, the first of Mozart's attempts in the *opera seria* medium, in many ways resembles works by Gluck then in vogue; it tells how brave King Mithridates vainly fought the Roman conquest of Asia Minor. This excellent, enthusiastically received score contained one duet, and a concluding quintet in which the survivors swore to seek liberty; the other numbers were calculated to let the principals display their vocal powers in arias, formal in the Italian manner and often moving, particularly Mithridates's in Act III.

The success of *Mitridate* led to another commission for Milan the following year: *Ascanio in Alba*, a dramatic serenade in two acts, gracefully blending ballet and cantata into a form not unlike the English masque. This commission came from Empress Maria Theresa herself through Count Firmian, as part of the wedding celebration of Archduke Ferdinand and Princess Maria of Modena. Words for the classic story were by a Salzburg poet, the Abbé Giuseppe Parini; the plot relates how Venus established Ascanius, son of Aeneas, as leader of the city of Alba (forerunner of Rome), and also how she acquired a wife for him, Sylvia by name. A cyclical method is used with certain charming themes recurring, generally as choruses. The simplicity of this story does not imply that the music is vocally easy; rather the sunny atmosphere assures a happy ending.

While intrigues prevented Mozart from immediately

following up his Milan success with another, his meeting there with Jean Georges Noverre was to lead a few years later to a Parisian ballet, *Les Petits Riens*. Meanwhile he was commissioned to compose a one-act dramatic serenade for the Archbishop of Salzburg. Premiered on March 14, 1772, *Il Sogno di Scipione* harks back to "The Dream of Scipio" from Cicero's poem; in a dream, Scipio shows proper perception in preferring the rewards of the Goddess of Constancy to those of the goddess Fortune. Transposition for the theater was made by Metastasio, that supreme librettist of the age, who had about thirty of his works set by such composers as Handel, Gluck, Haydn, Hasse, and Jomelli. Lorenzo Da Ponte, librettist of Mozart's later Italian operas, while deprecating the inevitable happy ending to which his predecessor was partial, conceded that Metastasio's works (setting a reaction to the French tragic style of the seventeenth century) were the most beautiful he knew.

Mozart's last opera written for Milan, *Lucio Silla* (K. 135), showed the composer a master of the *opera seria* form. Metastasio's libretto for this three-act work, revised by Giovanni di Gamerra, suggests an early wave of romanticism; this is reflected in the music, particularly in the airs of Giunia, who resists Sulla, winning the right to marry her beloved Senator Cecilio as Sulla renounces his dictatorship.

We must remember that Mozart could not generally exert as much control over his librettists as could Verdi, for example. Mozart pretty much had to take what was given to him, and though sometimes he could enforce minor changes in the libretto, his job was to turn out music; in many circles, musicians were regarded as only a step higher than valets. As we have seen, commissions generally came to the composer from reigning princes when the theme had been decided upon and approved, and more often than not the libretto was ready for him. Mozart was known to be a rapid composer and frequently received a commission at the last minute.

For Mozart's ninth opera, *La Finta Giardiniera,* the librettist was Gluck's famous collaborator Ranieri di Calzabigi (who also rebelled against Metastasio's happy endings, though he provided one here). This text was adapted by Coltellini, who set the action near Turin. First produced in Munich in 1775, the work was revised for a performance in German, at which time much of the original was misplaced. Revived today, it probably receives a more farcical production than Mozart intended. The story concerns the search of Sandrina for her former beloved, Belfiore, who had believed her dead, in fact by his own hand; there are a number of intrigues, but the third-act curtain finds six of the seven characters happily united, with only the local potentate disappointed.

Another Metastasio-based work, also produced in 1775, with the modest facilities of Salzburg, was *Il Re Pastore,* resembling in different ways both *Bastien* and *Ascanio.* Within a bucolic frame Alexander the Great persuades Amintas, rightful heir to the throne of Sidon, to assume the crown without relinquishing his beloved Elisa. Music and text remind us that for Mozart, as for Handel, it was a short step from opera to dramatic oratorio, and but another to sacred works.

We know of Mozart's years of friction with Archbishop Colloredo, ending with his resignation. He composed no more operas until *Zaide*, begun in 1779 to a libretto by his good friend Schachtner, who had provided *Bastien*. Turkish scenes and themes were much the rage throughout Europe and especially in Vienna, due to the proximity of the Turkish Empire—once a great menace, but now rather a peaceful neighbor. Unfortunately this German *Singspiel* remained uncompleted and unperformed until after Mozart's death, though some of its ideas were incorporated into *Entführung*. It was during these same years that Mozart became interested in the Masonic movement, an interest that bore extraordinary fruit in a number of his compositions, particularly a decade later, when "Egyptian" and Masonic lore were woven into that master fairy tale *Die Zauberflöte*. Eight pieces were completed at this time as incidental music for Gebler's *Thamos, König in Aegypten*. The play was not a success (though in some ways it foreshadows Goethe's *Egmont*); Mozart was sadly disappointed, as he greatly favored the interludes and chorus he had written. The powerful use of the key of E-flat and its related minor offers striking evidence of the composer's ability to characterize without extended musical development.

Once again there was a hiatus during which no operas came from Mozart's pen. When he resumed with *Idomeneo,* his thirteenth theater work, the poet was Varesco. The story of the creation of Mozart's later operas and of their literary, dramatic, and musical problems is well known; suffice it to reiterate that by this stage in his career he had demonstrated his mastery of those elements he was to use to ever increasing effect. Not the least of his achievements was the skillful weaving of a sure fabric of development with devices of Italian, German, and French origin into a unified entity, appropriate in its own style to the theme at hand. This specific aptitude and universal applicability of Mozart's operas grew from careful attention to detail, cosmopolitanism guided by taste, and above all a respect for individuals and humanity, a sense of the drama of life.

Mozart after Mardi Gras

BY FREDERICK W. STERNFELD

Beethoven once remarked that he could never have written an opera on such frivolous subjects as those of *Figaro* and *Don Giovanni*. It is certainly true that themes of heroic conjugal love and passionate hatred of tyranny have no place in *Le Nozze di Figaro*. Mozart and his librettist went so far as to delete from Beaumarchais's comedy most of the elements of social satire, thus making of *Figaro* an *opera buffa* in which the light touch is never lacking. Mozart wrote his father on June 16, 1781: "There should be as little frivolity in an *opera seria* and as much seriousness and solidity as there should be little seriousness in an *opera buffa,* and more frivolity and gaiety." It is a measure of Mozart's greatness that while his *opera buffa* bows to contemporary social expectations, it abounds in sparkle and laughter. Beethoven's Leonore, disguising herself as Fidelio in order to liberate her prisoner-husband, has no place for frivolity in her high moral purpose. But Cherubino, masquerading as a girl, adds a delightful touch to Beaumarchais's "Mad Day"; it is reminiscent of the laughter and gaiety associated with the masked balls that traditionally punctuated the carnival season. In the history of the theatre it recalls the tradition of the Comedy of Masques, well known from Shakespeare's comedies and countless operas of the eighteenth century, later echoed in the role of Octavian-Mariandel in *Rosenkavalier*.

The happy middle period of Mozart's development is marked by this awareness of his audience's expectations and his willingness to gratify them. The series of his works that begins with the *Entführung* in 1782 and culminates in *Figaro* in 1786 is endowed with a serenity and happiness that bring to these compositions the quality of *Gesellschaftsmusik*, that is to say, music written to satisfy the anticipations of society, chiefly that layer of society functioning as patron of the arts. Mozart's urban audience demanded entertainment during the long winter season, and the stage was its first love, then as now. A composer might profit from this situation by writing operas—Italian operas—if he wished to satisfy the sophisticated and cosmopolitan taste of the aristocracy and the upper middle classes. But as Mozart was, with Shakespeare, "not of an age but for all time," his works were also characterized by a profundity that went far beyond their immediate significance. The height of the season, immediately after Christmas, was gay with masked balls and stage spectacles. But the oncoming of Lent caused a temporary cessation of this pleasurable living, and theaters were closed. Here our modern organized concert life begins, since concerts given at regular intervals and open to a subscribing public were a means of passing the time. The first European series, the *Concerts Spirituels,* were founded in Paris in 1725 and had their counterpart in the *Akademien* of Vienna, as the concerts performed there in the Lenten season were called. For these concerts it was not uncommon to include a number of arias from the operas, a new symphony, and a piano concerto (with Mozart himself as soloist); in addition, the composer would show his prowess as an improviser at the piano.

The receipts from Lenten concerts became a substantial part of Mozart's annual income; they were more lucrative, in fact, than the operas, which commanded equal pay in Austria, Bohemia, and Italy, namely 100 ducats or 450 gulden.* This fee precisely Mozart received for *Figaro* in Vienna in 1786, for *Don Giovanni* in Prague in 1787, for *Die Zauberflöte* (paid to him by Schikaneder) in 1791. Occasionally the payment was greater, as in the case of *Così Fan Tutte,* for which the composer received an exceptional fee of 900 gulden. But the Vienna production of *Don Giovanni,* which was but a revision of the Prague premiere, netted only the half fee of 225 gulden. Opera commissions were not easy to come by; they required more rehearsal time than concerts, and their production en-

* Equivalent to $202.50 in eighteenth-century currency. Mozart paid $207 a year rent; his highest salary was $370 a year.

tailed considerably greater expense. From the composer's point of view, moreover, concerts offered the advantage that a good deal of the music need not be newly composed, except perhaps in the case of a new piano concerto.

In the Lenten seasons of 1784, 1785, and 1786 Mozart gave a series of three concerts (*Akademien*) in each season, and to these series we owe a number of the piano concertos of that period. Fourteen concertos were composed between 1782 and 1786, as against only two full-length operas, *Entführung* and *Figaro*. The income from the concerts also varied, averaging conservatively 500 gulden per concert, 1,500 gulden per season. In 1785 Leopold Mozart reported to his daughter Marianne, "Lebrun and his wife have offered three remarkable concerts; the first netted 1,100 gulden, the second 900 gulden and the third 500 gulden. Your brother has made 559 gulden in his concert." That is to say, one concert brought in more money than either *Figaro* or *Don Giovanni,* though only one new work in the form of a piano concerto appeared on the program. Nor should we assume that Mozart's income as composer-pianist was restricted to concerts arranged by him, for he frequently appeared as a guest in the Lenten concerts of music societies or of aristocrats or other virtuosos, notably singers. His happiness over the acclaim that invariably greeted him is apparent in his own letters and in those of his father. We also sense it in his music, particularly in those fourteen concertos, which are at the same time the finest and most profound "social music" that

Vienna's classical period produced. But viewing the receipts in contemporary perspective it must be remembered that, then as now, an operatic star earned considerably more than an operatic composer. Mozart's first Susanna (Nancy Storace) received an annual salary of 4,500 gulden plus expenses, which included lodgings. By contrast, Gluck's salary as court composer was 2,000 gulden. Mozart was even less successful when he succeeded to Gluck's post in 1787, for the salary was thereupon reduced to 800 gulden, over half of which the composer had to disburse in rent.

The income from the Lenten concerts, then, while not enormous, was clearly Mozart's main source of income. In spite of this, Mozart ceased to offer any *Akademien* after the series of 1786, the year in which *Figaro* was produced, and the composition of piano concertos also showed a marked falling off. By the summer of 1788 the writing of symphonies, too, came to a halt. Why, then, did Mozart deprive himself of his most lucrative source of income, as well as of the opportunity to dazzle his listeners with his brilliant playing? The answer to this enigma hinges on the development of Mozart's creative genius, which, in his middle period, culminated in *Figaro*. It hinges, too, on the relationship between the artist and his public, not to say his clients. The financial records have no interest here except as a gauge to show Mozart in step with the times, and they reveal that he worked in some conformity with the fashions and taste of his day.

Up to the turn of the eighteenth century the dreamer-artist, driven to create for posterity because his contemporaries did not appreciate him, was unknown in Western civilization. The artist worked as a craftsman to satisfy a demand and was paid accordingly, like a bootmaker, tailor, or carpenter. Raphael and Palestrina, Canaletto and Handel, did not produce on speculation, though this is not to say that their work did not go beyond the satisfaction of their patrons' taste or requirements. Shortly before 1800 we begin to perceive another type of creator, the artist of the Romantic period, who is still with us: the misunderstood genius, of whom Schubert, perhaps, is the earliest true example in music. The clashes between Beethoven and his aristocratic patrons are too frequent to be ignored, however much they may be exaggerated by anecdote. Beethoven, it is true, wrote for commissions and even rewrote his opera *Fidelio* the better to satisfy his Viennese audience. Yet the conscious importance he attaches to himself as creator, and as a prophet who must consider his inner calling rather than his public, separates him by a considerable gulf from his teacher Haydn. Socially Mozart occupies the same intermediate position between these two composers that he does chronologically: he is less content to serve his aristocratic masters than Haydn and at the same time less ruthlessly stubborn in asserting himself. Beethoven was implacable in his determination to maintain his freedom; Mozart was willing to compromise, at least up to and including *Figaro*.

The middle period of Mozart's career began in 1781–

Playbill for the first performance of Mozart's *The Marriage of Figaro,* Monday, May 1, 1786

The Burgtheater in Vienna, scene of the world première of Mozart's *Figaro*

Above: Act I of the Metropolitan Opera's production of *The Marriage of Figaro* with Judith Raskin (Susanna), Teresa Stratas (Cherubino), Hermann Prey (Count Almaviva), and Mariano Caruso (Don Basilio). *Below:* A model of Oliver Messel's set for Act I of the Metropolitan Opera's current production of *Figaro.*

Right: Oliver Messel's sketch of a costume for Susanna. *Below:* Lisa Della Casa as the Countess Almaviva, Cesare Siepi as Figaro, and Judith Raskin as Susanna in Act II.

Louis Mélançon

Paul Seligman

Above: The Oliver Messel set for Act II. *Below:* The finale of Act II showing Judith Raskin, Cesare Siepi, Lisa Della Casa, Hermann Prey, Mariano Caruso, Gladys Kriese (Marcellina), and Elfego Esparza (Bartolo).

Above: Oliver Messel's sketch of a costume for the Countess. *Below:* Judith Raskin and Lisa Della Casa in the letter duet from Act III.

Above: The marriage ceremony in Act III. *Below:* Oliver Messel's set for Act III.

Right: Sketch of a costume for Figaro by Oliver Messel. *Below:* Cesare Siepi as Figaro pretends to woo the Countess, Judith Raskin, whom he recognizes as Susanna in disguise during Act IV.

Louis Mélançon

Paul Seligman

Above: A model of one version of Oliver Messel's set for Act IV. *Below:* The finale of Act IV showing Joy Clements (Barbarina), Stratas, Esparza, Kriese, Lorenzo Alvary (Antonio), Della Casa, Prey, Raskin, Siepi, Caruso, and Gabor Carelli (Don Curzio).

82 when he resigned his position in Salzburg to move to Vienna (much against his father's wish), when the *Entführung* was produced, and when he married Constanze (again against his father's judgment). On the surface it might seem that these events constituted a declaration of independence and that Mozart broke with authority and became the free-roving hero-artist of the Romantic period. But this supposition would be far from the truth. Mozart left Salzburg for Vienna because he felt the latter city offered better scope for his work. He exchanged a provincial for a cosmopolitan patronage that offered superior opportunities for an operatic composer and pianist. Vienna to him was a "Clavierland," and when the Lenten time closed the theaters, he offered *Akademien* at which his genius shone and was applauded. Box-office receipts reveal that in this period Mozart's public and patrons were with him. There proceeded at the same time a quiet, inner development that was eventually to crystallize in the dark, demoniac music of his third and last period, anticipated in the 1780's in his study of the works of Johann Sebastian Bach and the composition of several of the six string quartets dedicated to Haydn. (By the publisher's payment of a mere 450 gulden for all six quartets we perceive that chamber music was by no means so lucrative as the writing of operas or pieces for symphony concerts.)

Obviously, when we consider Mozart's success with his public, we must focus on the operas and the piano concertos that appealed to a large, wealthy audience, eager for display and brilliance. Here we find the essential Mozart of the middle period, with only flashes of that other tragic Mozart apparent in the demoniac and poignant String Quartet in D minor which heralds *Don Giovanni*. Indeed, from the time of this opera (1787) until *Die Zauberflöte* and the *Requiem* (1791) the dark touches dominate. No longer was this *Gesellschaftsmusik,* nor could it be. For the development of Mozart's art was such that to satisfy the aristocracy, whose plaudits were synonymous with financial success, was of consequence no longer. Hermann Abert, in his classic revision of the biography of Mozart by Jahn, sums it up admirably:

> Now, at the end of his life, the flight of his genius leads him into a new country, no longer dominated by a single layer of society (no matter how highly educated), but dominated by the conscience of the creative artist, a country on whose horizon one already perceives the dawn of Beethoven's art. No wonder the audience did not follow him.

We have in this passage the reasons why Mozart offered no more subscription concerts of his own to the Viennese public after the production of *Figaro* in 1786.

The charm of the works of the middle period lies in the fact that they are so utterly pleasing without ever being shallow, the product of a composer hoping to succeed with the public yet confident of the unique stamp of his individuality. Mozart's dramatic and instrumental works were at that time never conceived *in abstracto;* they were tailored for such individual performers as an Osmin, a Figaro, himself (or one of his favorite pupils) as pianist. He paid careful heed to what his Viennese audience—and others—wished, namely virtuoso singing in the opera and virtuoso playing in the concert hall, and the vicissitudes of the Vienna season, whether theaters were open or closed, were also carefully considered. There hangs in the Kunsthistorisches Museum of Vienna a famous canvas by Peter Brueghel, "The Battle Between Carnival and Lent," symbolizing the seasonal changes to which the social and, in consequence, the concert life was subject. At this period, between his twenty-sixth and thirtieth years, Mozart seems to have had the poise to accommodate himself to the fluctuations of Viennese social manners and the individual deadlines imposed on him. Concerts and commissions fed his art without dominating or oppressing him. How different the story of the *Requiem,* for which he accepted an advance payment of 450 gulden (the ubiquitous financial figure in the Mozart records) and which he was not able to complete, so preoccupied was he with the idea of death and the premonition of his own early passing.

In *Figaro* we have a unique synthesis, for its profound and subtle quality did not disturb the essential structure of light plot and melodious songs. As a matter of fact, one of the reasons for the opera's popularity was the very nature of the plot, which, in general outline and specific articulation, was familiar to a goodly portion of the public. As we all know, its suspense and resolution rely heavily on the device of the masquerade. The Count's jealousy hinges on Cherubino's disguise as a girl in the boudoir of the Countess (providing the complications of the Finale of Act II), and the general reconciliation at the end of the opera is brought about by the mutual exchange of clothing between the Countess and Susanna. Add to these dramatic ingredients the stock figure of the clever servant-barber who rights all wrong, and we have the greater part of the story. Indeed, the clever valet, whether he be Mozart's Figaro or Leporello or Rossini's barber, is another form of the Spanish *gracioso,* who traces his descent to Lope de Vega. (In this connection it is noteworthy that the action of all of these operas takes place in Spain—an operatic Spain, to be sure.) Whether Cherubino is dressed as Barbarina's cousin or Susanna as the Countess (or Don Giovanni as Leporello), the dramatic situation is in the tradition of the masked ball, with which Mozart was well familiar not only as composer but also as participant. One of his duties as court composer required that he write compositions of dance music for the masked balls of the carnival season. His own fondness for these occasions and the problems of proper costuming are topics frequently touched upon in his letters to his father.

That Mozart's audience expected the usual ingredients of the Comedy of Masques in an *opera buffa,* even though the premiere of the opera did not always take place in carnival time, goes without saying. The prevailing European tradition of the Comedy of Masques accounts for the

similarity between Beaumarchais's *Mariage de Figaro* and
Sarti's popular comic opera *Due Litiganti* (with libretto by
Goldoni, one aria of which is quoted in *Don Giovanni*).
In Sarti's opera, too, we have disguises, a Count who is
enamored of the Countess' maid, and a clever *gracioso*,
the bailiff Masotto, who rights everything and himself
marries the maid. Now, Beaumarchais's *Figaro*, though
written in 1776, was not performed until 1784, whereas
Sarti's *Due Litiganti*, later so popular in Vienna, had its
premiere in Milan in 1782. It cannot be assumed, there-
fore, that one work influenced the other, but the general
tradition of the Comedy of Masques, well known to the
public and frequently used as a pattern by authors, is in-
herent in both plays.

Here was a piece to the public taste, a comic plot with
multiple complications within the traditional framework
of the *buffo finale*. Yet its historical significance is that
Mozart's genius created a work of lasting influence. The
public liked masquerading, frivolity, and the comedy finale
with as many singers as possible on the stage, and Da Ponte
and Mozart bowed to its wishes. But what Mozart's audience received into the bargain was more abiding: it was
the stuff of which immortality is made.

The Happy Ending

BY FRANK J. WARNKE

There can be no doubt that *The Marriage of Figaro* is one of the great triumphs of the comic spirit in Western art. From beginning to end it is a thing of laughter and delight, ranging in its effects from the broad to the delicate, from comedy of situation to the most perceptive comedy of character. But almost none of the commonplaces about the nature of comedy will serve to explain *Figaro*'s effect on the listener. Psychologists and literary theorists have found the basis of our experience of the comic in several different human impulses—the pleasure we take in feeling superior to our fellow men or in observing their discomfiture, the satisfaction we derive from seeing antisocial behavior brought again under the rule of society, the emotion we feel in witnessing minor incongruities of situation or attitude. *Figaro* has elements that appeal to all these impulses, but its essential nature lies somewhere beyond them. We are amused at the Count's exposure but feel no contempt for him; Figaro's schemes evoke our sympathetic attention as well as our laughter; the pathos embodied in the Countess's two great arias lifts her altogether out of the sphere of what we normally consider comic character. The ending of the opera, above all, catches our emotions and compels us to identify with the characters to a degree that makes any kind of detachment impossible.

The infinite depths of emotion in Mozart's score do not, however, conflict in any way with the general comic effect of the opera. It maintains to the end an unsurpassed artistic unity, composed equally and simultaneously of the laughable and the touching. *Figaro* has almost nothing to do with either satire or farce, those two forms of comedy which turn up so frequently in our experience. All elements of cruelty or malice have been purged away to leave only a comedy of the purest sort, a work of art as profound, as human, and as wise as tragedy.

The last act demonstrates to perfection the qualities that define pure comedy. A triumph of humorous confusion, it exploits the richest possibilities of situation comedy; at the same time it is a masterpiece of musical characterization. Fortunately for the perfection of the opera, its ending is happy for all concerned. Anything less than an entirely positive conclusion, any broken or embarrassed comic scoundrels left on the scene, would disturb us, for the last act has engaged our emotions too thoroughly with all its characters. Susanna's ineffably tender "Deh! vieni, non tardar," her delicate but moving duet with Figaro, above all the sublime moment at which the Countess forgives her errant Count—these have brought us too close to reality, have sounded too clearly the Shakespearean note of universal reconciliation, to allow us to bear anything but general happiness in the comic world. Only the Countess's serene affirmation, "Più docile sono, e dico di sì," can serve as fit conclusion, and after that nothing will do but that the people of the opera's world—Figaro and Susanna, Count and Countess, Cherubino and Barbarina, even Bartolo and Marcellina—must all be granted the happiness of shared love.

The ending is appropriate and satisfying; the lovers are brought together, the Count gains his lady's forgiveness, and the Countess, at least for the present, regains her Count. But as they go together to the feast that is to celebrate their common joy, one senses a curious pattern of fulfillment, as if that joy were something vaster than anything in their finite world of intrigue, infidelity, and fragile mortality. There may be a clue in the fact that the conclusion of *Figaro* is strikingly like that of ancient Greek comedy.

Greek comedy, as anthropologists and historians tell us, originated as the ritual worship of Dionysus, god of the vine and ultimately of the fertility of the earth. At some point in the dim preclassic past, the wild annual orgies of drunkenness and promiscuity that did honor to the god yielded to symbolic representation—ritual dramatic per-

formances in which a hero, attacked by his enemy, tri-
umphed over him, and in which his triumph was celebrated by feasting and a *gamos,* or general union of the
sexes. Thus was the earth's continuing fertility symboli-
cally confirmed and, to the primitive mind, assured. In
the classic comedy of Aristophanes and Menander, the
Dionysiac pattern, although expressed in submerged and
infinitely more sophisticated form, can still be perceived.

In yet more sophisticated form it can be perceived in
The Marriage of Figaro. Lovers of the opera from Hippolyte Taine to Ernest Newman have commented on the
omnipresence of the sex motif in *Figaro.* The opera deals,
after all, with a marriage, and Susanna and Figaro, for all
their wit and aplomb, are deeply in love. The Count is
prodigiously attracted by each and every woman; Cherubino, in his boundless susceptibilities, seems almost an
adolescent and innocent parody of his experienced lord.
The page's first aria, "Non so più cosa son, cosa faccio,"
with its breathless evocation of youth's vulnerability to
love, enunciates a theme explored by the opera in an infinite variety of ways. Even the aging Marcellina is in her
own way the servant and victim of Eros. In such a context,
the final pairing of lovers in *Figaro* suggests with great
force the mythic pattern of Greek comedy.

But the opera is not a simple restatement of ancient
fertility myth, any more than it is simply a satire with
political implications, like the Beaumarchais play from
which it is derived. It is a highly intellectual product of

a complex society, given shape by an intensely individual genius. It makes a statement about human life—the force of desire, the fragility of virtue, the necessity for forgiveness—in a profoundly moral way. But like those comedies of Shakespeare's middle period which are the closest literary equivalents to its spirit—*As You Like It, Much Ado About Nothing, Twelfth Night*—*Figaro* presents its mature wisdom through a dramatic form that recapitulates, however unconsciously, the primitive impulse toward the worship of the fertility principle. The peculiarly serene joyfulness of its score expresses the deep moral vision of its composer, that human beings, for all their weakness, imperfection, and folly, are capable of laughter, love, and the godlike act of forgiveness. At the same time it expresses something less intellectual and perhaps more universal: the creature's joy in the creation, the sense of earth's eternal renewal, and man's participation, through love, in that renewal. Like all comedies, *Figaro* is a criticism of life; like all great comedies, it is more a celebration of life.

The Twilight of the Almavivas

BY WILLIAM WEAVER

The lover of opera cannot imagine a Figaro grown old;
Mozart and Rossini have made their hero too immortal for
that. We can imagine him in another time, another garb,
but he would still be young, ardent, foxy, and indomi-
table. Yet the barber's original creator was not so kind to
him; Beaumarchais couldn't leave his masterpiece alone.
And late in his life, besieged by personal troubles he had
lost the spirit to overcome, the author wrote a third play
about the Almavivas and their entourage, *La Mère Coupable*. This is not listed as a *comédie* like its two predeces-
sors but is ominously called a *drame*.

Beaumarchais himself must have been aware of the
weakness of this third play. The other two have long,
pugnacious prefaces in which he takes issue with all his
attackers. But here, the shorter introduction has all the
earmarks of an apology. The times are more serious now
(*La Mère Coupable* was produced, in its final version, *le*

16 Floréal, 1797), so plays and playwrights must be more serious, too.

"Oh, my fellow-citizens," the introductory remarks conclude, "you to whom I offer this play! If it seems weak or unsuccessful to you, criticize it, but without insulting me. When I wrote my other plays, for a long time I was abused for having put into the theater that young Figaro whom you have since come to love. I was young then, too; I laughed at the abuse. But as we grow old, our spirits sadden, our character becomes somber. Try as I may, I can no longer laugh when a rogue or a villain insults me. . . ."

Alas, the play *is* weak and unsuccessful and all too easy to criticize: a mechanical melodrama where the sly, plausible villain is introduced into a good family, making mischief, until he has set husband against wife and master against servant; then at the last, with the usual melodramatic twist, the faithful old family retainer uncovers the plot and all is saved; the young people can marry, the old people are reconciled, and the faithful servant refuses a reward for his good deed, because "his reward will be to die in his master's house."

This would be bad enough if it were just any play, but it isn't: the old couple are Lindoro and Rosina, the faithful servant (who refuses money!) is Figaro. And Susanna is there, too, doddering around the stage, wringing her hands and restoring her faint mistress with smelling salts. Just as Figaro is no longer the devilish intriguer he once was, so Countess Rosina is no longer the independent spirit who fought back against her scheming guardian and her straying husband, ready to put on her maid's clothes or open her jalousie to a stranger.

No, life has caught up with them all. The Countess has lost her innocence as well as her spirit, and for twenty years she has been weeping and despairing because of a secret crime (she yielded once to Cherubino and the result is Léon, the young swain of *La Mère Coupable*); the Count despises his pretended son and refuses to let the boy marry his ward, Florestine (who, as the villain knows, is the Count's illegitimate daughter). The Count is too busy for philandering these days; he has money problems (the family is living in Paris so that he can legally lift the entail from his Spanish holdings) and family responsibilities.

The younger generation, too, is not what it should be. Léon is a far cry from the Count as a young man; instead of seizing the girl he wants, he can only bewail his fate and expect time to take care of him. And Florestine's lack of enterprise would never have done in the old Seville days.

Like the playwright, the Almavivas are concerned with politics. The Count, though he is still proud and worried about the succession of his name and titles, has the servants call him *"monsieur"* instead of *"monseigneur"* in deference to the progressive country where they are living. He also has a fine bust of Washington in his study. In the *dramatis peronae* young Léon is described as a young man *"épris de la liberté, comme toutes les âmes ardentes et neuves. . . ."* In fact, the evening before the play opens, he has scored a considerable success with a speech he made, which only a timely interruption of the villain prevents him from repeating to his mother and Florestine, and the audience.

Figaro, grown more honorable with the years, scorns money, but the Count—once so prodigal—puts it above all else. The final tragedy in this tragedy-packed play seems to be that the villain, after he has been unmasked, may make off with three million *livres d'or,* which the Count entrusted to him. The recovery of the money takes up an entire act. Earlier, when the Count, stricken with remorse, fears that his still-beloved Rosina will die, he can think of nothing more heartfelt to say than, "Susanna, a million to you if you save her."

From the tedious opening scene (where, in a clumsy bit of exposition, Figaro and Susanna remind each other of what has happened in the past twenty-odd years) to the finale with its weak moral ("enough is gained in a family when an evildoer is driven out of it"), the play has not a moment of wit or life; Figaro's monologues are stage rant; the Countess's tears are glycerin, not salt. The plot would be unworthy of Scribe at his worst, and even poor Piave could equal the dialogue.

Fortunately composers—usually so prompt to seize on a bad play—have wisely avoided this one, and it has fallen into deserved oblivion. [However, Darius Milhaud's opera on the subject was performed in Geneva in June 1966.]

We reread it now only as an example of an author's poor judgment; but the example proves that a great creation, a true character like Figaro, is a kind of Golem or Frankenstein monster. The author can create him but cannot kill him off again. And Figaro, his head full of plots and his voice full of song, lives on to mock the final effigy his author called by his name.

From Revolution to Romance

BY ALFRED FRANKENSTEIN

Once it was a document of revolution: today it is a romantic comedy of love-intrigue. In its own epoch it was,
in Paul Bekker's admirable phrase, an "opera of critical
realism": now we esteem it for its romantic vivacity, its
comic freshness, its music of moonlight and garlands.

Thus *The Marriage of Figaro,* like countless other works
of art, proves the past to be as unpredictable as the future,
proves the artistic judgment of each era to be channeled
and conditioned by circumstances forever changing. Yet
some works survive all fluctuations of attitude and emphasis, because they have in their inmost fabric something
eternally new.

Such, to the highest and most preeminent degree, are
the masterpieces of Mozart, those of opera and those of the
concert repertory.

The story behind *The Marriage of Figaro* is long and
complicated. The work goes deep into the heart of its

time and rides the crest of the historic forces which, within a very few years, were to push the shaky aristocratic society of that day into the discard. It symbolizes vast social change and in that sense is a peculiarly fitting opera for our own moment.

A sketch of that background, of Mozart's daring to sing what might not then be spoken, would be interesting and revealing; but space limitations prevent its being told here. Perhaps its most important manifestation, from our point of view, is the characterization in music of which Mozart is a rare and perfect master. Gone are the days when an aria for the soprano heroine might be cobbled for the bass villain, when music for one opera might be transferred to another. Each Mozartian personage lives in his own music, and each Mozartian opera lives in its own atmosphere. Mozart's concept of naturalism in characterization has many important and fascinating aspects, not the least of which is that he thinks of the human voice almost solely in terms of soprano and bass-baritone, as is clearly revealed in his assignment of roles in *The Marriage of Figaro*.

Mozart is unique among the opera composers of his time in being a past master of every manner of musical expression. He knew how to make music as few have ever done before or since; and his incomparably plastic, supple, and masterly polyphonic technique raises his ensembles to a symphonic height without equal in the whole range of opera. Herein is one of the sources of Mozart's infinitely varied appeal to the modern audience. His music, a perennial freshet of invention, forever creative, totally innocent of labor or contrivance, creates order. To appropriate to *Figaro* what Nietzsche said of a very different opera, "This music is precise. It builds, it organizes, it completes." It is thus a peculiarly apt spiritual freshener for a disorderly time; and like all the music of Wolfgang Amadeus Mozart, it might fly as its standard the profound esthetic principle which Nietzsche sets forth as first of all:

"What is good is easy; everything divine runs on light feet."

Mozart among Us

BY MAX RUDOLF

M, a man in his mid-thirties, lives in a walk-up apartment in a brownstone house on Manhattan's West Side. He moved there recently and, indeed, has been changing apartments at the rate of one a year. People in his neighborhood do not know much about him. He came originally from Boston, where his father, also a musician, had a good position. The son had been less successful and for this reason moved to New York about ten years ago. At first, music circles were very much interested in M, but he is not the kind of person to make friends easily, and he certainly does not know how to associate with the right people. It is remembered that he was a child prodigy twenty-five years ago; M still enjoys the reputation of being an unusually successful master as far as the technique of composition is concerned, but his works do not display real feeling and, above all, his taste in music is poor. For this reason, he has never achieved real fame like other success-

ful composers of our day. Strangely enough, he is well
liked in San Francisco, where his operas are performed
with great success and his concerts are always sold out and
meet with genuine enthusiasm. Unfortunately, the public
in New York consider him second-rate.

About a year ago, M borrowed money for a trip to
Toronto; indeed, one of his friends who was driving up
offered him a seat in his car. They did not especially like
him in Toronto: no position was offered to him as he had
hoped. Since his return, he has been sickly and does not
look healthy. Apparently he does not eat as he should. His
wife is ill and frequently goes to Atlantic City. Actually
they have no money for this extravagance and have to bor-
row from everyone. In general, the M's have been living a
disorderly kind of life. He is probably too lazy to give
lessons, or he cancels them so that students will not study
with him. He feels that writing music is more important.
When Toronto failed, M wanted to go to London, where
Covent Garden had invited him to write an opera and to
produce it there; but there was no money for the voyage.
He managed to go to a recent music festival in Mexico
City. Naturally, he did not receive financial assistance
from the government, as did a few outstanding American
composers, so the poor devil had to pay for the trip. They
say that he had to pawn his last belongings.

At this moment, there is a musical comedy on Broadway
for which he wrote the music. This has become a hit show
but, after all, the music is not important; it is the ex-

cellent book which makes people buy tickets. Maestro M is said to be so badly off that he has applied to the assistant choirmaster at one of the large churches in Manhattan. He even has offered to work without pay just to show his ability, but how could he be considered since there are so many outstanding musicians in the field?

In a few words, this is an entirely realistic picture of Mozart's life in Vienna in 1791, the year of his death.

Note:
Boston: Salzburg	*Mexico City: Frankfurt*
San Francisco: Prague	*Atlantic City: Baden*
Toronto: Berlin	*Church: Vienna Domkirche*
	Musical Comedy: Magic Flute

Incidentally, London is not fictitious, because Covent Garden actually invited Mozart during the last year of his life.

Index

Abduction from the Seraglio, The (Die Entführung aus dem Serail) (Mozart), 2, 60, 76
Ah! Signor!, 5
Akademien (Vienna), 115, 116
Alten, Bella, 57
"Antonio" (character in *Figaro*), 5, 101
Apollo et Hyacinthus (Mozart), 105
Aprile, Giuseppe, 90
Aprite, presto, aprite, 5
Aprite un po' queqli occhi, 6, 12, 17, 42
Arias in *Figaro*, dramatic role of, 17-18
Arne, Michael, 87
Artois, Count d', 73
Ascanio in Alba (Mozart), 108
Attwood, Thomas, 95

Background of *Figaro*, 1-3
"Barbarina" ("Fanchette") (character in *Figaro*), 4, 6, 102
Barber of Seville, The (Beaumarchais), 2, 50, 60, 70, 71, 73
"Bartolo, Dr." ("Bartholo") (character in *Figaro*), 4, 5, 28, 51, 100
"Basilio, Don" (character in *Figaro*), 3-5, 21, 22
Bastien und Bastienne (Mozart), 105-106

"Battle of *Figaro*, The" (Lingg), 75-80
"Bazile" (character in *Figaro*), 102
Beaumarchais (Pierre Augustin Caron) *The Barber of Seville*, 2, 50, 60, 70, 71, 73
  La Folle Journée, 71
  life of, 65-74
  The Marriage of Figaro, 2, 8, 9, 13, 40, 45, 52-53, 66-68, 70-73, 98-99, 123
  La Mère Coupable, 68, 74, 129-133
Beethoven, Ludwig van, 36, 60, 113, 118
Benucci (opera singer), 82
Brandt, Marianne, 56
Breuer, Robert, "The Court Jester," 65-68
"Brid'oison" (character in *Figaro*), 102-103
Brownlee, John, 3
Buffo finale in *Figaro*, 31, 32, 35, 37
Buona Figliuola, La (Piccinni), 87
Burgtheater (Vienna), 2
Bussani, Dorotea, 81-85
Bussani, Francesco, 81-85

Calzabigi, Ranieri di, 110
Caron, Pierre Augustin, *see* Beaumarchais
Casti, Abbate Giambattista, 77, 84, 93

Cavalieri, Laura Caterina, 82

Chamfort, Sébastien Roch Nicholas, 72

Characters in *Figaro*, pronunciation of names of, 3

Che soave zefiretto, 6

"Cherubino" ("Chérubin") (character in *Figaro*), 3-6, 8-10, 17, 18, 25, 26, 48, 54, 55, 57, 61-63, 102

Cigna-Santi, Vittorio Amadeo, 107-108

Cinque, dieci, venti, 4

Clairval (Italian stage idol), 70

"Clarinet in *Figaro*, The" (Kozma), 58-64

Colloredo, Archbishop, 111

Coltellini (adapter), 110

Comic spirit in *Figaro*, 124-128

Common man in Mozart's works, 47

Concerts Spirituels (Paris), 115

Contessa, perdono!, 7

Cosa sento?, 4

Così Fan Tutte (Mozart), 42, 60, 83, 106

Costumes in *Figaro*, 97-103

"Count Almaviva" ("Le Comte Almaviva") (character in *Figargo*), 3-7, 10-11, 21, 22, 24, 25, 27, 28, 39, 43, 47-48, 55, 100

"Countess" ("La Comtesse") (character in *Figaro*), 3, 5-7, 13-14, 17, 24, 25, 39, 40-41, 43, 48, 55, 63, 100

"Court Jester, The" (Breuer), 65-68

Crudel! perchè finora, 5

"Curzio" (character in *Figaro*), 3

Cushing, Mary Watkins, "Mooncalves," 54-57

Cymon (Arne), 87

Da Ponte, Lorenzo, 2, 9, 14, 22, 31, 32, 40, 77-79, 81-85, 109

Memoirs, 82

Il Ricco d'un giorno, 77

"Da Ponte and the Bussanis" (Harris), 81-85

Deh! vieni, non tardar, 6, 13, 17, 42, 55, 125-126

Denner, Johann Christoph, 58, 59

"Despina" (character in *Così Fan Tutte*), 83

Devin du Village (Rousseau), 105

Didur, Adamo, 55

Don Giovanni (Mozart), 33, 39n, 60, 80, 91

Dove sono, 6, 14, 40, 48

Downes, Edward, "A Tender Irony," 8-15

Due Litiganti (Sarti), 123

Eames, Emma, 3, 55

Eccomi a' vostri piedi, 7

Einstein, Alfred, 15

Ensembles in *Figaro*, dramatic role of, 18, 21, 23

Entführung aus dem Serail, Die (The Abduction from the Seraglio) (Mozart), 2, 60, 76

Expanded version of *Figaro*, 2

Farrar, Geraldine, 55

Faust (Gounod), 56

"Figaro" (character in *Figaro*), 4, 5-7, 11-12, 28, 39, 43, 55, 69, 100-101, 129-133

"*Figaro* Dressed for Paris" (Raeburn), 97-103

"*Figaro's* Perpetual Motion" (Griffith), 16-30

Finarolo (singing master), 90

Finta Giardiniera, La (Mozart), 106, 107, 110

Finta Semplice, La (Mozart), 106, 107

Fischer, Johann Christian, 87

Flute in *Figaro*, 59

Folle Journeé, La (Beaumarchais), 71

Frankenstein, Alfred, "From Revolution to Romance," 134-136

"Frederick" (character in *Mignon*), 56-57

"From Revolution to Romance" (Frankenstein), 134-136

Gabrielli-Del Bene, Adriana, 82

Gainsborough, Thomas, 87

Gamerra, Giovanni di, 109

Gebler, *Thamos, König in Aegypten,* 111

Gente, gente! all'armi!, 7

German, first major operas in, 2

Giovani liete, 4

Giovanni, Don (Mozart), 33, 39n, 60, 80, 91

Gluck, Christoph Willibald von, 22, 45-47

Glyndebourne Festival, 1934 (England), 3

Goethe, Johann Wolfgang von, 8, 86

Griffith, Katherine, "Figaro's Perpetual Motion," 16-30

Guardasoni (opera producer), 95

Hamlet (Shakespeare), 43

Handel, George Frederic, 45

"Happy Ending, The" (Warnke), 124-128

Harris, Lloyd, "Da Ponte and the Bussanis," 81-85

Hastings, Baird, "The Road to *Figaro*," 104-112

Hautbois (instrument), 58

Haydn, Franz Joseph, 91

Hempel, Frieda, 57

Ho perduta, L', 6

Human being in Mozart's works, 46-49

Human Tragicomedy (Scherr), 35-38

Idomeneo (Mozart), 112

Joseph II, Holy Roman Emperor, 2, 78, 79, 89

Keller, Gottfried, 48

Kelly, Michael (Michael O'Kelly), 82

 life of, 86-96

 Reminiscences, 78

Kerman, Joseph, "Marriages in *Figaro*," 38-44

Kierkegaard, Søren, 10

King Lear (Shakespeare), 43

Kozebuch (pianist), 91

Kozma, Tibor

 "The Clarinet in *Figaro*," 58-64

 "Master of Human Insight," 45-49

Lange, Aloysia, 82

Leopold II, Holy Roman Emperor, 84-85

Lingg, Ann M.

 "The Battle of *Figaro*," 75-80

 "Meet Marcellina," 50-53

Lion, Henri, 69

Louis XV, King of France, 70
Louis XVI, King of France, 65-66,
    71-73
Lucio Silla (Mozart), 109

Magic Flute, The (Die Zauberflöte)
    (Mozart), 40, 42, 60, 106, 111,
    120
Mandini, Stefano, 82
"Marcellina" ("Marcelline") (char-
    acter in *Figaro*), 3-6, 26-28, 49,
    50-53, 101
Maria Theresa, Holy Roman Em-
    press, 1, 108
Marie Antoinette, Queen of France,
    66, 73
Marriage of Figaro, The (Beaumar-
    chais), 2, 8, 9, 13, 40, 45, 52-53,
    66-68, 70-73, 98-99, 123
"Marriages in *Figaro*" (Kerman),
    38-44
"Master of Human Insight"
    (Kozma), 45-49
Méchant, Le, 68
"Meet Marcellina" (Lingg), 50-53
Meistersinger von Nürnberg, Die
    (Wagner), 47
Memoirs (Da Ponte), 82
Menotti, Gian-Carlo, *The Old Maid
    and the Thief*, 18
Mère Coupable, La (Beaumarchais),
    68, 74, 129-133
Mesmer, Dr. Anton, 106
Metastasio, Pietro, 105, 109, 110
Metropolitan Opera House (New
    York), 2, 3
"Michael Kelly" (Nettl), 86-96
Milhaud, Darius, 132
Mitridate (Mozart), 1, 107, 108
"Mooncalves" (Cushing), 54-57
Morland (pianist), 87

Mozart, Wolfgang Amadeus
    career of, 119-123
    childhood of, 1
    death of, 1, 121
    father of, 1
    finances of, 115-117
    individualism of, 118-119
    life of, 75-80, 137-139
    personality of, 46
    wife of, 91
    See also specific works
"Mozart after Mardi Gras" (Stern-
    feld, 113-123
"Mozart Among Us" (Rudolf), 137-
    139
"Mozart's Wedding Symphony"
    (Sternfeld), 31-37
Music in *Figaro*, dramatic role of,
    18-30
Music of Mozart, 135-136

Napoleon I, Emperor of the French,
    9, 73
Nettl, Paul, "Michael Kelly," 86-96
Newman, Ernest, 127
Nietzsche, Friedrich Wilhelm, 136
Nilsson, Christine, 57
Non più andrai, 5, 17, 62
Non so più cosa son, 4, 10, 55, 103,
    127
Nordica, Lillian, 3
Noverre, Jean Georges, 109

Oboe in *Figaro*, 58, 59
Oca del Cairo, L' (Mozart), 106
"Octavian" (character in *Der
    Rosenkavalier*), 54-57
O'Kelly, Michael, *see* Kelly, Michael
Old Maid and the Thief, The
    (Menotti), 18

Opera buffa, 1, 31
Orchestra, Mozart's use of, 60
Orsini-Rosenberg, Count, 76-79, 89
"Oscar" (character in *A Masked Ball*), 57

Paisiello, Giovanni, 73, 93
  Il Re Teodoro, 77
Panizza, Ettore, 3
Parini, Abbé Giuseppe, 108
Park Theater (New York), 2
Passerini (singing master), 87
Patience (Sullivan), 30
Paul, Grand Duke, 73
Peretti (singing master), 87
Pergolesi, Giovanni, 45
Petits Riens, Les (Mozart), 109
Pian pianin le andrò più presso, 6
Piccinni, Niccolò, *La Buona Figliuola*, 87
Pinza, Ezio, 3
Porgi, amor, 5, 14, 40
Puccini, Giacomo, 60

Raeburn, Christopher, "*Figaro* Dressed for Paris," 97-103
Rauzzini, Matteo, 87
Re di Ponto, see Mitridate
Re Pastore, Il (Mozart), 110
Re Teodoro, Il (Paisiello), 77
Requiem (Mozart), 120, 121
Reszke, Edouard de, 3
Rethberg, Elisabeth, 3
"Revolutionary Figaro" (Stedman), 69-74
Ricco d'un giorno, Il (Da Ponte), 77
Ricevete, o padroncina, 6
"Road to Figaro, The" (Hastings), 104-112

Rosenberg, Count, *see* Orsini-Rosenberg, Count
Rosenkavalier, Der (Strauss), 45, 54, 56, 60
Rousseau, Jean Jacques, *Devin du Village*, 105
Rudolf, Max, "Mozart Among Us," 137-139

St. Giorgio (singing master), 87
Salieri, Antonio, 75-80, 89
Sarti, Giuseppe, *Due Litiganti*, 123
Sayão, Bidù, 3
Scalchi, Sofia, 56, 57
Scenery in *Figaro*, 97-99
Schachtner (librettist), 111
Scherr, Johannes, *Human Tragicomedy*, 65-68
Schiller, Friedrich von, 86
  Don Carlos, 8
Schuldigkeit des ersten Gebotes, Die (Mozart), 105
Scotti, Antonio, 55
Se vuol ballare, 4, 17, 61
Sembrich, Marcella, 55
Seraglio (Mozart), 42
Shakespeare, William, 43, 49, 128
Sheridan, Richard Brinsley, *School for Scandal*, 8
"Siébel" (character in *Faust*), 56
Singspiel (Mozart), 111
Sogno di Scipione, Il (Mozart), 109
Sono io stesso saltato di li, 5
Stedman, Jane W., "Revolutionary Figaro," 69-74
Sternfeld, Frederick W.
  "Mozart after Mardi Gras," 113-123
  "Mozart's Wedding Symphony," 31-37

Stevens, Risë, 3
Storace, Nancy, 94, 95
Storace, Stephen, 94-95
Story of *Figaro*, 4-7
Strauss, Richard, *Der Rosenkavalier*, 45, 54, 56, 60
Sullivan, Sir Arthur, *Patience*, 30
"Susanna" (Suzanne") (character in *Figaro*), 3-7, 12-13, 17, 18, 24-28, 39, 43, 51-52, 55, 101

Taine, Hippolyte, 127
"Tender Irony, A" (Downes), 8-15
Thamos, König in Aegypten (Gebler), 111
Tutto tranquillo e placido, 64
Twilight of the Almavivas" (Weaver), 129-133

"Urbain" (character in *Les Huguenots*), 57

Varesco (librettist), 112
Vedrò mentr'io sospiro, 6, 11
Vendetta, La, 4
Venite, inginocchiatevi, 5
Verdi, Giuseppe, 49
Via resti servita, 4
Voi che sapete, 5, 10, 55

Wagner, Richard, 46, 47, 49, 60
Warnke, Frank J., "The Happy Ending," 124-128
Weaver, William, "The Twilight of the Almavivas," 129-133
Works by Mozart, 104-112

Zaide (Mozart), 111